T0170362

Only Here for a Visit

www.penguin.co.uk

Only Here for a Visit

*A Life Lived to the Full – from Sporting
Glories to Wild Stories*

ALAN BRAZIL

CORGI BOOKS

TRANSWORLD PUBLISHERS
Penguin Random House, One Embassy Gardens,
8 Viaduct Gardens, London SW11 7BW
www.penguin.co.uk

Transworld is part of the Penguin Random House group of companies
whose addresses can be found at global.penguinrandomhouse.com

Penguin
Random House
UK

First published in Great Britain in 2020 by Bantam Press
an imprint of Transworld Publishers
Corgi edition published 2021

A CIP catalogue record for this book
is available from the British Library.

ISBN
9780552177818

Typeset in Garamond MT Std by Jouve (UK), Milton Keynes.
Printed and bound in Italy by Grafica Veneta S.p.A.

The authorized representative in the EEA is Penguin Random House Ireland,
Morrison Chambers, 32 Nassau Street, Dublin D02 YH68.

Penguin Random House is committed to a sustainable
future for our business, our readers and our planet. This book
is made from Forest Stewardship Council® certified paper.

For all the great players I have played with and against. Sadly, many have passed.

Contents

Hoops Dreams

Sometimes I feel like I've lived two separate lives. Indeed, there are people who listen to my show on talkSPORT and have no idea I played football professionally. It happens a lot with sportspeople who hang up the boots/ clubs/racquet/bat and take up the microphone instead. I suppose it shows that I've been able to completely rein-vent myself, which I should take as a compliment. But once upon a time, I was a pretty handy footballer. And when I was a kid growing up in Glasgow, my whole life was the game.

I was only seven when Celtic's Lisbon Lions became the first British team to win the European Cup, in 1967, but I have hazy memories of gathering around a tiny black-and-white TV to watch it. That was when I learned that grown men cry as well as children. It was just such an incredible story: a bunch of childhood friends, all brought up within 25 miles of Celtic Park, who had come through junior and senior football together and become one of the greatest sides European football had ever seen. Celtic won nine straight league titles from the 1965/66 season, having won only four over the previous forty years. But once upon a time, Billy McNeill, Jimmy Johnstone and

Stevie Chalmers were just little kids like me, playing with a tennis ball in the street and dreaming of playing for the Hoops.

Our house was just down the road from Hampden Park. The first game I saw there involved the once mighty Queen's Park, who were then in the Second Division and played their home games at the national stadium. That was a strange occasion, standing in this cavernous ground with more than 100,000 seats, hearing my own cheers echoing off the roof. But when Celtic were playing there, that meant the Hoops were in another cup final. Not that I had tickets when I was a little kid. Instead, me and some pals would take a ball with us and sit on the hill. We'd only be able to see the Celtic end, which was Hampden's East Stand and didn't have a cover on it. If there was a big roar and we saw people jumping up and down and clouds of dust rising up, we'd know that Celtic had scored. If there was a more distant roar, we'd know that the other team had scored, which was normally Rangers and never a good thing.

But the game that really stands out from that era happened three years after the triumph of the Lisbon Lions, when Celtic played Leeds in the European Cup semi-final second leg at Hampden (Celtic manager Jock Stein had switched the tie from Celtic Park, to make it as intimidating as possible for Don Revie's English league champions). I was still in shorts, so there was no way my parents were going to let me go to the game. But as luck would have it, my pal John Reilly lived just off Aikenhead Road and his garden backed on to the wall at the Celtic end. Just before kick-off, we stuck a ladder against the wall and about twelve of us climbed up it and scrambled into the ground.

Billy Bremner scored a corker to put the English champions ahead on the night, before John Hughes and Bobby Murdoch put the tie to bed for Celtic. The official attendance that day was 136,505 – a record for the tournament – but that was just paying punters. If you accept that we weren't the only fans who bunked in, the true figure might have been closer to 140,000. My heroes lost the final against Holland's Feyenoord, which was as devastating as the victory over Inter Milan three years earlier was beautiful.

From the time I could talk, I was nagging my mum to get me cup final tickets. Eventually she caved and bought two for the 1970 League Cup final, between – you guessed it – Celtic and Rangers. The problem was, we were in the wrong end (not in the terraces, but on the wrong side of the halfway line) and Rangers' sixteen-year-old striker Derek Johnstone scored the only goal of the game. I got terrible pelters that day, from Rangers and Celtic fans. The Celtic fans were having a go at me for sitting with the enemy, and the Rangers fans were having a go at me for being the enemy. About twenty minutes before the end, a steward wandered over and said, 'Look, you'd better go.' My mum grabbed me by the ear and off we marched towards the exit.

My first Celtic away game was against Dundee in the Drybrough Cup, which was a quirky, short-lived tournament for the four highest-scoring teams in the top two divisions. It was a midweek game and I remember shouting from the front door, 'See ya! Just off to the football!' and bolting before my mum could ask any questions. I got a bus to the centre of Glasgow, before catching a train to Dundee. There were a lot of older guys I knew on the train and that was the first time I drank beer. I hated the taste of it.

Those older kids could get a bit rowdy, so I thought the best thing I could do was stay away from them, because I didn't want to get into any trouble. Big mistake. The game went to extra-time and Dixie Deans scored the winner for Celtic. But because it wasn't an important game and Celtic didn't bring many fans, the Dundee supporters fancied their chances and there were fights galore. I was walking back to the station with my head down, trying not to make eye contact with anyone, when I turned a corner and saw about a dozen Dundee fans ahead of me. Suddenly, I wished I hadn't given my mates the slip.

The Dundee fans started asking where I was from and I quickly decided that rather than attempt a conversation, I should leg it. A few of them gave chase but I was very fast in those days and left them for dead. At the station, I hid behind a bus and waited for things to calm down a wee bit before creeping on to the platform and catching the last train back to Glasgow. All my mob were on the train and they'd all had a great time. While I was running for my life, they'd been having scuffles and punch-ups and loving every minute of it.

When I got back to Glasgow I tried to sneak back into the house, but my mum and dad had waited up for me. Only when it started to get late had they found out that the game was in Dundee and not Glasgow. The fact that I stank of whisky, which I'd been showered in when Deans scored the winner and again on the train home, didn't help my situation. My mum smashed me over the head and my dad gave me a good old-fashioned clip round the ear. That was par for the course in those days. Some kids would have got it far worse.

Every night I dreamed of playing at Hampden for my beloved Celtic, in those beautiful green-and-white hoops. Not a day went by when I didn't play football on the street, on the fields behind King's Park Secondary School or, if we were in mischievous mood and the janitor wasn't about, on the well-manicured hockey pitch, which resembled the hallowed turf of Wembley.

Because I grew up middle class – my mum and dad owned grocery shops, worked every hour God sent and owned their own house – in a part of Glasgow called Simshill, Catholics mixed with Protestants and a lot of my mates were Rangers fans. But if you were a Celtic fan, chances are you pretended to be wee Jimmy 'Jinky' Johnstone. I did, too, at least out loud, because I fancied myself as a tricky attacking player. But in my head I was the skipper Billy McNeill, not only because he lifted the European Cup in 1967, but also because he attended the same church as me, Christ the King on Carmunnock Road. I could never quite believe he was in the same room as me and would spend the entire service staring at him. And when I discovered that Billy had family living on my road, those games of street football took on an extra importance. I imagined that a cousin might be looking out of his window, see me in action and get straight on the phone: 'Billy, I think I might have found you the new Jimmy Johnstone . . .'

It wasn't just Celtic legends who lived near me. Some of my pals lived around the corner to Alex Ferguson, who played up front for Rangers in the late 1960s. After playing football in Linn Park, I'd walk past Fergie's house on Farne Drive on my way home, pick the flowers in his front garden and chuck them over my shoulder. I look back now and think how weird that was, ruining a man's garden just because he played for Rangers. I only stopped after a neighbour told my mum what I was up to and she gave me a backhander.

When I was little there was a brand-new primary school about 100 yards from my house, but that was for Protestant kids. Because I was a different kind of Christian, I had to toddle down the hill in my shorts to the Catholic St Mirin's school. The Protestant lads would barge into me and give me stick, but I was quite big for my age and they got it back, don't worry about that. Secondary school was a place called Holyrood, which was one of the biggest schools in Scotland. There were kids from the Gorbals, Pollokshaws, Pollokshields and Toryglen, forty of them to a class. It must have been a nightmare for the teachers, but they must have been doing something right because Holyrood produced plenty of talent. Jim Kerr and Charlie Burchill from the band Simple Minds were in my class, and I used to go skating with Charlie a lot. Also in my class was a guy called Gerry McElhone, who went on to manage the band Altered Images and whose brother Johnny, who was a few years below us, played guitar for Texas. Paddy Crerand, who won the European Cup with Manchester United in 1968, had also gone to the school, as would the comedian Frankie Boyle and Fran Healy, the lead singer of Travis.

You knew you were a half-decent player if you played for your year, because there was some serious talent. And you had to be tough, because when we played against Protestant schools, chances were it would all kick off. Some of these schools were in proper working-class areas of Glasgow and the kids would try to intimidate us middle-class Catholic lads from Holyrood. Midweek games, against schools like Kingsridge in Drumchapel, where Andy Gray and Celtic great Danny McGrain are from, could be particularly raucous. There would be hundreds of kids around the pitch screaming blue murder, and opposition players trying to kick us up in the air. There were skirmishes all over the pitch, just as there were skirmishes all over the streets of Glasgow.

Walking home from a Celtic game wearing green and white was fraught with danger. But I didn't think of it as scary or dangerous, I thought of it as a thrill and an adventure. I didn't really care, as long as I got to see my team. When it came to the Old Firm, that Catholic–Protestant edge made it the best game of football in the world, which is an inconvenient truth for some people. In fact, it wasn't just an edge, it was pure hatred. That hatred of the other team was part of a lot of people's DNA, and I had as much of it as anyone else. Whenever Rangers got close to Celtic's goal, I'd feel sick to the stomach.

The way I'm describing it, you're probably thinking Glasgow was a terrible place to grow up. But I wouldn't swap my youth for what's happening now. I got clipped by my parents and the teachers gave us the leather strap. But I never saw it as a problem, because I probably deserved it. Now, parents and teachers aren't allowed to hit their kids, but what's replaced it? Kids swearing at their parents, hitting their teachers, and a complete lack of respect for anyone in a position of authority. And out on the streets, kids are stabbing each other to death daily. That can't possibly be an improvement and it's going to be our downfall. Discipline at home and at school was what made boys into men, and we don't have enough of it now.

That said, sectarianism caused misery for a lot of adult Catholics. My brother is seven years older than me and remembers when pubs had signs on their doors saying 'No Dogs. No Irish' – and by 'Irish', they meant 'Catholic'. One of the first questions a prospective employer would ask was, 'What school did you go to?' And if you named a Catholic school, that was your chances gone. So when I was fifteen, my brother left Glasgow for Australia, because he couldn't get a job in the city.

Rangers legend and talkSPORT colleague Ally McCoist tells me that in some Glasgow families now, one brother might support Celtic and another might support the Bluenoses. That never could have happened when I was a kid, so maybe things are beginning to ease up. As for me, that fierce sense of rivalry has never left me despite the fact I've lived in England for forty-five years. I've got a lot of very good friends from the 'other side', people like Ally, who scored lots of important goals against Celtic. We're not bitter or nasty about the Celtic–Rangers rivalry, we're able to have a laugh and a joke about it. Of course, that's how it should be. But when a game kicks off, that friendship is put to one side.

I remember watching one Old Firm game in an executive box with Tommy Gemmell. (I once asked Tommy what it was like scoring in a European Cup final, and he replied, 'Which one?' I'd forgotten that as well as scoring in the 1967 final, he also scored when Celtic lost in 1970.) When Celtic scored their second goal, we both went to the front of the box and started waving at the Rangers fans, to wind them up. Tommy was a European Cup winner and I'd played thirteen times for Scotland, but we were like a couple of little kids again.

In 2007, my brother, who's still a massive Celtic fan and involved in the Perth supporters club, came home for a visit and we watched an Old Firm game at Ibrox. Celtic were terrible and lost 3-0, and afterwards we went to a bar in the south side of the city, near where we went to school. On our way there we got some terrible abuse from Rangers fans, even those who weren't at the game.

That was horrible. My brother had come all the way from Australia and I'd really wanted him to have a great day. Instead, the Hoops got battered by the Gers and he learned that sectarianism was still alive and well.

At Glasgow Airport that evening, I was sitting at the bar nursing a Guinness, feeling dejected and minding my own business, when a load of English Rangers supporters piled into the place. As soon as I saw them, I said to the guy next to me, who was also a Celtic fan, 'This could be interesting . . .' They were singing 'Rule Britannia' and giving me dog's abuse, and I was pretending I couldn't hear them. But eventually I cracked and said to this guy next to me, 'Have you got your scarf in your bag?' He was shitting himself and told me to ignore them. But I kept nagging, so he gave me his scarf and I put it on. When one of these Rangers fans got right in my face, I got up and started giving them some verbals back. It was like being transported back in time, to when I was a kid.

Suddenly, two cops appeared from nowhere, got me by the scruff of the neck, took my pint off me, gave this guy his scarf back and marched me on to the plane. They plonked me down in a seat at the front, told me that if they heard another peep out of me they'd arrest me, and ordered the attendants not to give me another drink. I was sitting on the plane on my own for about forty minutes. I remember thinking to myself, 'Christ. Almost getting into fights with Rangers fans at your age. What are you doing? Ridiculous.'

*

When I was about twelve, club scouts started coming to the house to talk to Mum and Dad. And it was about that time that I had trials for Celtic Boys Club and was asked to play for them. That was a proud day. I was a smart kid and did well at school, but that all meant nothing now. I was going to be a footballer, come what may.

Although the Boys Club wasn't Celtic's official academy, they trained at Celtic's Barrowfield training facility and would nurture a lot of Hoops and Scotland greats, including Charlie Nicholas, Paul McStay and Roy Aitken, who was my under-16s captain. On training nights we had to show up in our green blazers and grey slacks (if we didn't, we didn't get in), which made me an easy target for groups of Protestant lads. But going home with my badge ripped off my blazer and my trousers covered in holes from fighting just made me even prouder to wear the green of Celtic.

My first big game for Celtic Boys Club was an under-14s final against Rangers Boys Club, on Glasgow Green. In those days Glasgow Green's football pitches were all red ash, but hundreds of people would come and watch any game between Celtic and Rangers, even if it involved a bunch of kids. Some of my team-mates were cowed by that kind of gladiatorial atmosphere, but I thrived on it. People on the touchline swearing at me and trying to trip me up just made me more determined to win. While some of my team-mates didn't fancy venturing beyond the halfway line, where the Rangers fans were massed, I was screaming for the ball and surging forward whenever I got it. I was also flying in with dangerous tackles, just to rile their fans. On that particular day, we won 7-1. But we didn't always have it our own way. A year later we got beaten 5-1 by a Rangers feeder team called East-ercraigs, which was made up of boys from all over the city. The side I played against included Jim Melrose, who had a long career in England and a spell at Celtic, and Davy Reid, who was at Leeds for a while. But win or lose, I didn't stop banging in goals.

When I was fifteen, I got fed up with being moved all over the pitch and decided I wanted to play up front. I had always been fast and skilful, with an eye for goal, and I thought striker was the best position for me and the team. I was right. In my under-16s season I scored sixty-two goals, a league record that I believe still stands. And when you set goalscoring records for Celtic Boys Club, you expect Celtic to sign you. Had they asked me to sign, I would have bitten their arm off. But they never did. So when Ipswich Town's Scotland scout George Findlay asked me if I'd like a trial, I wasn't going to turn him down.

Many years later, I was playing for Scotland at Hamp-den Park when a director from the Scottish FA said to me, 'Son, how did we let you slip through the net?' I couldn't give him an answer, and I still don't know for sure. What I do know is that my time at Celtic Boys Club wasn't all goals and glory. When I was thirteen, I was sexually assaulted by a man called James Torbett.

Torbett was in charge of Celtic Boys Club and there-fore a respected figure in both the Catholic and football community. In those days there wasn't the same safeguarding as there is today. As far as parents were concerned, if someone was a pillar of the community, and connected to Celtic Football Club, they were safe around children and beyond reproach. When they sent us off to play for Celtic Boys Club, they didn't imagine we could be in any danger. They just thought we were playing football and having fun. Sadly, they were wrong.

I knew something wasn't quite right about Torbett the first time I met him. When you're twelve years old, it's sometimes difficult to put your finger on why you don't like someone. But I wondered why this man in charge of one of the most famous junior clubs in Scotland didn't seem to have a football past and never did any coaching. I was suspicious of the fact that he bought lads burgers after games and gave them lifts home. He'd also invite us to his house, where he'd ply us with biscuits and bring out boxes of toys for us to play with, even though we were far too old for them. And I could never understand why it was such a seedy little place, given that he was meant to be a wealthy businessman.

On one occasion, before a big European tournament, he invited a big gang of us round and I remember him touching and kissing some of the lads, before dishing up ice cream for everyone. I thought, 'What on earth is going on here?' That same afternoon, I was sitting on the sofa in the living room, feeling bored and thinking about leaving, when Torbett came in and shut the door behind him. He sat down next to me, started kissing my head and put his hand between my legs. I recall that I was wearing my Boys Club blazer and grey slacks, and

13

can still picture the leer on his face. I froze for a couple of seconds, then a couple of lads walked in, at which point I jumped off the couch, ran to the bathroom and locked myself in. My heart was thumping like crazy and my head was swimming. I thought to myself, 'Will he come after me? If I jump out of the window, will I injure myself? Have I imagined the whole thing?'

After a few minutes, I bolted from the bathroom, grabbed my mate Davey Gordon and told him we were leaving. I ran all the way to the bus stop, with Davey trailing behind me. I didn't tell him what had happened. I didn't tell my parents either. How could I? They would have been confused and devastated. Just like me. I wasn't picked for the European tournament and stopped going to the club as often, which surprised my mum and dad. They'd say to me, 'You won't fulfil your dream of playing for Celtic if you don't go.'

It wasn't as if I was having nightmares, I just didn't want to be near him. I went from being the biggest football nut in Glasgow to someone who wanted to stay in all the time and do his homework. Incredibly, Torbett would sometimes phone the house, asking if I wanted to meet up for extra training sessions. He even asked if I wanted to meet up with him and some lads for a meal, promising ice cream. The shamelessness and arrogance take the breath away. I've never eaten ice cream since. Just the sight of it makes me feel sick.

Signing for Ipswich was one of the best things I ever did. But I can't help wondering how things might have turned out had Torbett not been involved in my life.

People still say to me, 'How come you never played for Celtic?' Maybe Torbett told the people who mattered at the club that I had an attitude problem. Maybe what happened had no bearing on Celtic not signing me. It's impossible to say either way. But something strange went on. And I never stopped dreaming of walking out at Celtic Park for a game against Rangers, before scoring the winner. 'Alan Brazil – Hoops Hero'. That's got a nice ring to it.

People still tell me how brave I was to speak out about my abuse at the hands of Torbett, but I might never have said anything had I not been compelled to. One day in the mid-1990s, long after I'd retired from football and when I was starting to find my feet in the media world, I received a phone call. When I picked up, there was a very troubled Scotsman on the other end, not making a great deal of sense. It was my old Celtic Boys Club team-mate Davey Gordon, who had been with me that fateful day at Torbett's house.

When he finally calmed down, Davey told me that the *Daily Record* had been trying to bring Torbett down for years, that he'd spoken to them for a story and had named me. I had no idea that Davey had suffered at the hands of Torbett. But it explained the silent bus ride we shared after escaping from Torbett's house. Davey must have sensed that Torbett had molested me as well.

What Davey told me was shocking. So that evening I discussed what I should do with my family. I remember saying to one of my daughters, 'I've got to do this.' And she replied, 'So do it.' I didn't want the *Daily Record* making up a pack of lies, but I also wanted to do it in solidarity with Davey and whoever else Torbett had abused. It made me sick to think how Torbett had been getting away with it for all those years, while those he'd abused had been suffering. I'd been lucky, in that I'd managed not to let what happened affect me too much. I'd reflected on it sometimes, but while it made me wary of people, I'd managed to get on with my life and thrive. But now I decided that Torbett should be locked up and his name should be all over every newspaper. If that meant my name being all over every newspaper as well, so be it.

This was before the internet had become widespread and when rumours didn't travel as far and wide. But when I started making enquiries, I soon realized that Torbett's nefarious activities had been the subject of hearsay for years. I even discovered that Jock Stein, on hearing of the accusations, had literally thrown Torbett out of the club. But Torbett had somehow managed to worm his way back in. So when the *Daily Record* reporter got in touch, I was ready to tell them everything. The story caused a huge sensation in Scotland and opened the floodgates. Frank Cairney, my under-16s manager, was also implicated. And two years later, Torbett and I had our day in court together.

On the opening day of the trial, a lad called James McGrory described how Torbett had abused him over a period of three years. Apparently, James had phoned the police after reading the story about me. Torbett had given James lifts home from training and taken him to the pictures and cafés. He'd even asked James to meet him for extra training. That sounded familiar. James hadn't told anyone because he was embarrassed and feared that no one would believe him. He'd also worried that Torbett would drop him from the team, just as he'd done to me.

On day two of the trial, it was my turn to give evidence. The cab driver who ferried me from the airport to the court told me to 'nail the bastard' and refused to take any money. When I got out of the cab, it was pandemonium. There were reporters, photographers and cameramen everywhere, and a couple of policemen had to escort me through the entrance, using their shoulders to part the crowd. The courtroom was packed, some people even sitting in the stairwells. And there, standing a few feet from me, was Jim Torbett. I stared straight at him and he was unable to hold my gaze for long. I felt strong and composed. I wasn't going to let this opportunity pass me by. I was adamant that he was going to get what he deserved. I was going to nail the bastard.

When the prosecution asked me to describe what Torbett had done to me, I looked straight into the jurors' eyes and told the truth. Then I was cross-examined by his defence barristers. They asked me if I thought Torbett's actions were accidental, to which I replied, 'I probably thought so at the time, but they sure weren't.' Because I'd been paid £10,000 by the *Daily Record*, they asked me if I'd spoken to them purely for financial gain. Obviously, I replied that that was nonsense. They also suggested that I'd made up the story, not only for the money but also to get back at Celtic for not signing me. I denied that as well. Other than that, the defence didn't go in as hard as I thought they might. And overall, I thought I'd performed well. When the judge told me I was free to go, I replied, 'No, I want to stay. Because I want to see his face as the questioning goes on.' The judge had no problem with that, so I watched the whole day's proceedings before flying back down to London.

The following week, Torbett was found guilty of acts of shameless indecency on three boys: me, Davey Gordon and James McGrory. I was elated. I was less pleased when the judge sentenced him to only two years. I thought he should have gone down for life, especially because I knew there must have been so many more who hadn't come forward. I was to be proved right. Twenty years later, Torbett, who had been living in California, was found guilty of sexually abusing three boys over an eight-year period and was sentenced to six years. One of his victims was only five. Six years was ridiculously lenient.

That same year, another former Celtic Old Boys chairman, Gerald King, was found guilty of sexually abusing children. And in early 2019, Frank Cairney was given a three-year sentence for abusing boys over a twenty-year period (although he only served half of that), and former Celtic Old Boys coach Jim McCafferty was jailed for six years for abusing teenagers over a twenty-five-year period. Given the extent of the abuse, people started wondering if Jock Stein had known and said nothing. Rangers fans even made up the song 'Big

Jock Knew', and unveiled banners saying the same at Old Firm matches. I don't know if those allegations are true or not. But given that so many people were involved – we still don't know if they've caught everyone yet, and I certainly remember that Torbett was always surrounded by the same four or five older boys – it's difficult not to conclude that some people at Celtic knew what was going on and covered it up.

For years, Celtic's official line was that the Boys Club was a separate organization, that they were not legally culpable and therefore wouldn't be issuing an apology. I understood why they took that position, because Celtic are a business and issuing an apology would have opened them up to maybe hundreds of compensation claims. But when I was a kid, I didn't see any separation between Celtic Boys Club and the 'big' club. I wore the same strip, my blazer had the same badge and I was watched by Celtic scouts. As far as I was concerned I was playing for Celtic's junior side, which was a stepping stone to playing at Celtic Park. To say there was no connection isn't right.

This terrible story should not be about business and lawyers and money. It should be about the victims and Celtic supporters, people who have loved the club all their lives and feel let down. Celtic did finally make some sort of apology in 2020, but the victims of the abuse deserve more than an apology, they deserve to be compensated. And it's not just Celtic who should be held to account. Did anyone in the Scottish FA know about it? Why has there not been a massive SFA inquiry?

Millions should be spent on finding out exactly what went on. The whole of Scotland might have been affected, just as it has been proved that there were clubs all over England with paedophiles on their staffs.

Since testifying against Torbett in court, I've received lots of letters and emails from former Celtic Boys Club players who were abused. I've even had a couple of phone calls from lads who are still too scared to come forward. Some just want to get things off their chests, others want me to help. It's frightening that those evil bastards destroyed the lives of so many people. It's also frightening that there were so many people involved – abusers and victims – and that it was allowed to go on for so long. I sometimes think about a guy called John McCluskey, whose brother George played for Celtic. They say that John was better than George and destined for great things. He was even dubbed 'the new Kenny Dalglish'. John suffered a bad injury as a young man and never fulfilled his potential, but he maintained it was Torbett who destroyed his life. Long before he suffered his career-ending injury, John turned to drink. I don't know where John is now, or even if he's still alive. I do hope he found some peace.

I've only hated one person in my life, and that's Jim Torbett. For as long as he's alive, there will be a shadow hanging over me. I saw him once at York Racecourse, before I saw him in court. He was making his way out, and as soon as I saw him I turned wild. I was screaming at him – 'You bastard! You bastard!' – and my mates had to grab hold of me. But I shrugged them off and pursued Torbett through the throng, my eyes glued to his white raincoat, which he'd always worn. However, after a few minutes, he was gone. I don't know what I would have done had I caught up with him. Maybe I would have smashed him in the face. Maybe I would have killed him. And he would have deserved everything he got.

Who knows how many kids would have gone on to be professional footballers had their lives not been ruined by Torbett. I've also heard about victims ending up in asylums and taking their own lives. Sometimes when I read the messages his victims send me, they will affect me. I'll thank my lucky stars that I got off lightly compared to others. I managed to recover from my ordeal and lead a successful life, but who knows why I was able to withstand it while others weren't able to cope. It's not something I want to think about too much. And when I read those messages, I feel impotent. I wish my evidence had led to Torbett rotting behind bars for the rest of his life. But I've done my bit, and having helped bring Torbett to justice, I want to move on.

2

The Blues

I was only sixteen when I joined Ipswich Town, but moving from Glasgow to Constable Country in Suffolk wasn't the culture shock I thought it might be. I was placed in digs in a beautiful little village called Bramford, not far from where I live now, and fitted right in. My landlady was a grumpy old girl who cooked terrible food and complained about the most trivial of things, like how quickly I came down her stairs and how I was wearing out her carpet, but at no point was I homesick. Throughout my life, I've never really felt out of place, which has enabled me to do so many things.

I was only on £14 a week as an apprentice, but so were the other lads. We'd get paid on a Thursday and it would all be gone by Friday evening. We were only kids and there wasn't much drinking, so we spent it all on clothes and betting instead. I damaged a knee cartilage in my first year, which I put down to the shuttle runs we did in training, nicknamed 'doggies'. They consisted of jumping in and out of these holes and springing up as we changed direction. Removing cartilage from a knee is a minor procedure nowadays, but back then it could quite easily have scuppered my dream of becoming a professional footballer. The fact that the surgery was successful, and I was given a second chance, made me even more determined to make it.

I came back firing on all cylinders in my second year. Our youth team played in the South East Counties League, which was dominated by the big London clubs, principally Tottenham, Arsenal and Chelsea. But Ipswich were the first team from outside the capital to win the league, in 1974/75, before retaining their title the following season. And with me banging in goals from all angles, we made it three titles in a row in 1976/77. That was the season I really grew up. One month I scored sixteen goals in four games – four goals in four consecutive matches – and at the end of the season I was voted South East Counties player of the year. Former Chelsea, Spurs and QPR star Terry Venables, who was Crystal Palace manager at the time, presented me with the trophy at the Café Royal in London.

But that season was also quite stressful, because despite all the wins, nobody knew if they were going to be signing pro forms at the end of it. Because Ipswich's youth system had been successful for a few years already, their first-team squad was quite young, which meant manager Bobby Robson didn't want too many more kids. And when the time came, only Terry Butcher, Russell Osman and I were chosen. That was heartbreaking. I was in the Cubs and Scouts as a little kid and had always loved that sense of togetherness. But suddenly, all these great lads I'd spent the last two years with had to disappear. Some tried their luck at other clubs, others went and got 'normal' jobs. I still see some of them in Suffolk, going about their business as builders or joiners.

My first professional contract was worth £55 a week, which I was absolutely thrilled with. But just because I now had a few quid in my pocket didn't mean I was excused menial jobs. In those days, apprentices doubled as skivvies. We had to clean the changing rooms and the older players' boots, wash the kit and even paint the stands in the summer. But we never had a problem with it; it's just the way it was. Now it's all changed, and not for the better. Not too long ago I had a row about it with PFA chairman Gordon Taylor. He kept saying, 'But apprentices are footballers, Alan, they're not cleaners and decorators.' But I thought it taught us discipline and respect for our elders.

On 14 January 1978, I made my first-team debut against Manchester United at Portman Road. We lost 2-1, and I only played two more games for the first team that season. But I was still only eighteen, and playing alongside some incredible players, so I thought I was on the right track. However, Bobby wasn't sure if I was going to make it long term and didn't know what to do with me. So one day he took me aside and told me he wanted to send me to America, to play for Detroit Express in the North American Soccer League (NASL). Express were co-owned by Coventry chairman Jimmy Hill and managed by a guy called Ken Furphy, who were both good friends of Bobby's. The plan was for me to play for them over the summer, try to find a yard or two of pace playing regular football, and then hopefully be offered a new contract with Ipswich on my return.

I was booked on a flight out of Heathrow the morning after the 1978 FA Cup final. I wasn't in Ipswich's squad to play Arsenal at Wembley, and neither was Eric Gates, because there was only one substitute in those days and Bobby picked Mick Lambert instead (to be honest, I felt more sorry for Robin Turner, who had scored in every round but was dropped for David Geddis, who had been playing regularly with me in the reserves). So on the morning of the final, me and Gatesy went to Hackney Wick Stadium and had a couple of bets on the dogs. Gatesy had the right hump, but eventually I swallowed my pride and said to him, 'Gatesy, I've got no money.'

'What do you mean you've got no money? You're going to America tomorrow.'

'I know. Can you help me out?'

Gatesy reached into his pocket and pulled out £40. That was all the money he had on him, and he gave it all to me.

A few hours later, local boy Roger Osborne scored the only goal at Wembley and promptly fainted, because he couldn't believe what he'd just done. And while I wasn't involved in the game, I was involved in the celebrations, which took place at the Kensington Royal Garden Hotel and went on until the early hours of the morning. But while the party was no doubt still going on, I was on a plane somewhere over the Atlantic, en route to New York.

When I landed at JFK Airport, there was no one there to meet me, as had been arranged. That afternoon, Detroit were playing New York Cosmos, so I needed to get to Giants Stadium in New Jersey, pronto. I went to the British Airways desk and said, 'Look, I'm playing soccer for Detroit at Giants Stadium, but no one has come to pick me up.' And the woman replied, 'Don't worry, Mr Brazil, we'll get you a helicopter.' Presumably because there was so much money swilling around the NASL and so many superstars were involved in it, players getting helicopters to games was quite normal. At least that's what she made it sound like. But after reaching into my pocket and feeling my £40, I suddenly said, 'Nah, I can't get a helicopter. I'm scared of flying.' So I got a yellow taxi all the way to New Jersey instead. Luckily, someone was there to meet me this time and paid the fare, otherwise I would have been stuffed.

New York Cosmos were the defending champions and had two World Cup-winning captains in their team, Brazil's Carlos Alberto and West Germany's Franz Beckenbauer. They beat us 2-0, but that didn't mean the boys weren't going to celebrate. After arriving in Detroit, we all went straight out, and as we walked into a nightclub called the Three Faces, 'Stayin' Alive' from *Saturday Night Fever* came on. I felt like John Travolta strolling into a disco with his mates. Bramford it wasn't. The place was buzzing, champagne corks were popping, everyone knew we played for the local soccer team, everyone knew everyone else, and I knew right then that I was going to have a great time in the States.

My apartment overlooked the Pontiac Silverdome, where we played our home games, and I had a cleaning lady and a porter who looked after my laundry and groceries. I was still a teenager, so that kind of stuff blew my mind. For the next few months I travelled all over North America – Dallas, San Diego, Denver, Chicago, Memphis, Houston, Vancouver, Minnesota, San Jose, Boston, Philadelphia, Anaheim, Fort Lauderdale – playing with and against some of the biggest names in world football. As well as Carlos Alberto and Beckenbauer, George Best, Rodney Marsh and Alan Ball were playing out there. Some of the star imports were past their best, but some of them were still on their way up, including my team-mate Trevor Francis, who was lightning fast, a great player and pro who gave me lots of encouragement. It was so exciting. I felt like a missionary, spreading the gospel of football to the American people.

When I first turned up we were getting crowds of 10,000 at the Pontiac Silverdome, which we shared with the NFL's Detroit Lions and which held 80,000. But towards the end of my time there we were getting over 20,000 for some matches. They were just desperate for a successful team in the city (their American football, basketball and baseball teams were pretty hopeless at the time) and we managed to win a fair few games. We won the Central Division to qualify for the play-offs and beat Philadelphia Fury in the first round to set up a game against Fort Lauderdale Strikers. I equalized to take the game to overtime before Best scored the winner. After the game, George said to me, 'Great left foot, pal. You've got a big chance of making it.' I couldn't believe it. George Best thought I had a great left foot! Those few words alone made the trip worthwhile.

The following day, we had a big farewell barbecue. The young American lads in the squad were always a bit pissed off that they were being overlooked for foreign talent like me, but I'd become very pally with them because they were more my age (Francis, who scored twenty-one goals in nineteen games that season, had already played almost three hundred games for Birmingham City and would become Britain's first £1 million player when he signed for Nottingham Forest the following season, so needless to say he looked after himself a bit better). That day we ended up getting smashed on Budweiser before one of the American boys pulled out this big bag of weed and offered me a smoke. I'd never smoked marijuana before, so I declined. But after a bit of persuasion, which I'm told is customary on such occasions, I caved and got stuck in.

Most of what happened next is a blur. But I do remember us being stopped on a highway and being thrown over the bonnet of a car by a police officer, like a criminal in an episode of *Starsky and Hutch*, and one of the cops pulling out a gun. After recovering from a fit of giggles, I explained that I was going home in the morning and showed them my flight tickets. Satisfied that this Brazil-shaped stain would soon be gone from their city, they put me in their car and drove me back to my digs. The last thing they said to me was, 'You're a lucky boy. Go home and don't come back.'

On the flight, I felt like I was dying. I slept most of the way home and it was only when we were circling over Heathrow that I was woken up by two of my Express team-mates, Newcastle goalkeeper Steve Hardwick and Norwich full-back Ian Davies. They were both in very good spirits and started telling me how much they'd earned in the US. Steve had saved $32,000 and was going to buy his mum a car and do a bit of work on the house; Ian had saved $29,000 and was going to get an extension and book a nice holiday. When they asked me how I'd done, I put my hand in my pocket and pulled out eighty bucks. At the time there were two dollars to the pound, so once I'd paid Gatesy back, I was left with nothing.

I found what I was looking for in America, namely a yard or two of pace, but spent most of the early part of the 1978/79 season on the bench before Bobby started putting me in his starting XI. I was still a teenager, but luckily my strike partner was Paul Mariner, who was as hard as they came. Then, in March 1979, Bobby picked me for the Cup Winners' Cup quarter-final second leg against Barcelona at the Camp Nou. When I first set foot in that stadium I couldn't get my head around how vast it was. At that time, Portman Road held about 35,000, but the Camp Nou's capacity was over 100,000. Only a few years earlier I'd been playing on red ash pitches at Glasgow Green.

We'd beaten them 2-1 in the first leg, with Gatesy scoring both our goals. That was a decent result, but their away goal meant that if Barcelona scored first in Spain, they could park the bus. And we knew what Barcelona were capable of on their own patch because some of the lads had played there a couple of seasons earlier, in the third round of the UEFA Cup. Remarkably, Ipswich won the first leg 3-0, but Johan Cruyff scored twice at the Camp Nou and Barcelona eventually won on penalties. Cruyff was no longer at Barcelona in 1979, but they didn't need him. A few minutes before half-time their rugged centre-back Migueli scored, we weren't able to nick one back, and they went through on the away goals rule.

Despite that disappointment, I now felt like an established member of the team and repaid Bobby's faith with a sackful of goals towards the end of the season. In the last six games I scored seven times, including two apiece against Bolton and Chelsea.

That was an extremely talented Ipswich team. We had Paul Cooper in goal; George Burley, Kevin Beattie, Terry Butcher, Russell Osman, Allan Hunter and Mick Mills in defence; John Wark, Arnold Mühren and Frans Thijssen in midfield; and me, Paul Mariner and Eric Gates up front. People are always telling me what a classic side it was, and they're exactly right. Every one of those players was a past, present or future international, and between them they made something like four thousand appearances for Ipswich.

Butcher and Osman were both hard as nails. Russell was two-footed and probably a better player than Butch, but Butch was a great header of the ball and blossomed into a formidable warrior. And, of course, they learned an awful lot from Allan Hunter, who won over fifty caps for Northern Ireland, and Kevin Beattie, who Bobby Robson thought was the best player he ever worked with. The fact that Kevin went by the nicknames 'Beast' and 'Diamond' tells you that he had everything. He could sprint like Usain Bolt, had springs in his heels and a cannon of a left foot. That he only won nine England caps is a mystery.

Kevin was also as daft as a brush. One time we had a game cancelled in Birmingham, and someone suggested we visit a leather factory down the road. I was so skint I couldn't even afford a pair of gloves, but the other lads filled their boots. Back on the bus, Kevin turned to me and said, 'Pelé' – that was my nickname, not because I played like Pelé, but because of my surname – 'look at this coat. I got it for a third of the normal price.' It would have been a beautiful coat, were it not for the fact that the arms barely reached past his elbows.

Like Kevin, George Burley had been at the club a few years before I arrived. George and I were always having a go at each other, because George was a big Rangers supporter. Apparently, his father was such a fanatical Bluenose that he wouldn't even eat Penguin biscuits with the green wrapper. Mick Mills was the perfect captain, very smooth and dapper. There was something of the David Niven about him. He smoked little panatella cigars, and whenever we went out for a drink he'd always have gin and tonic instead of beer. Johnny Wark was another Rangers fan, although Celtic were keen on signing him before he moved to Ipswich. Johnny was originally a centre-half, but when they moved him to midfield he became a goal machine. For a couple of seasons there wasn't a better attacking midfielder in the whole of England.

Bobby stumbled upon Arnold Mühren when he was in Holland looking at another player. Arnold had a wand of a left foot, and after he'd been at Portman Road a few months, Bobby said to him, 'Son, do you know anyone else as good as you back home?' Arnold replied, 'Yes, I know someone better – his name is Frans Thijssen.' So Bobby bought Frans as well. That Wark–Mühren–Thijssen combination was perfectly balanced. Johnny was a box-to-box midfielder who could score goals at one end and defend at the other, Arnold could pick a pass like few others I'd seen, and Frans wasn't afraid of putting his foot in but was also a great dribbler.

There were hardly any non-British players in English football in the late 1970s, so Arnold and Frans were really quite exotic. Their arrival also completely changed our style of play. Before Arnold and Frans, Paul Cooper would throw the ball out to George Burley or Mick Mills, they'd hit the centre-forward and I'd play off whoever that was, usually Paul Mariner. But the Dutch boys, who had been exposed to Johan Cruyff's philosophy of 'Total Football' (which demanded that everyone in the team had to be comfortable on the ball), wanted the full-backs to play it to their feet, before they fed it through to the front players.

It sounds basic now, but back then it was a breath of fresh air. It was only really after the two Dutchmen arrived that I understood how vital service from midfield was. Arnold and Frans gave everyone else the freedom to play, and it all gelled together superbly. Arnold in particular was so important to my game. He seemed to have a telepathic understanding of when and where I was going to run and the spaces to hit. He was a bit like an American football quarterback and laid on so many goals for me.

Instead of playing with wide men, Mariner and I would get in the channels and Johnny Wark and Eric Gates, the pocket rocket, would burst through the middle. Gatesy wasn't really a midfielder or a striker. Instead, Bobby created a new position for him, playing in the hole just behind the front two, and he scored some amazing goals playing in that role. We played a wee bit like Chris Wilder's Sheffield United do now. No one really knows what their formation is, because players are shifting positions throughout the game. They finished ninth in the Premier League in July 2020 with a small budget, so it obviously works, as long as you've got the players to do it well.

We were also a very fit team, even if Bobby's training methods were archaic by modern standards. Back then, pre-season was largely designed to get players fit again after four or five weeks of doing not a lot and eating and drinking what they liked. Bobby used to take us to the HMS *Ganges* base, a Royal Navy Training Establishment in Shotley, just down the road from Portman Road.

HMS *Ganges* had a 143-foot mast with a crow's nest at the top, although fortunately Bobby didn't have us climbing up and down that. Instead, he took us down to the shore establishment's running track and had us sprinting up and down a set of four hundred steps. Going down was bad enough but coming back up was agony. I'd wake up feeling like someone had been sitting on my legs all night. For the first ten days of pre-season, we wouldn't see a ball. And then we'd head over to Holland for yet more fitness training followed by a tournament. I was lucky in that I'd always been naturally fit (I was quite a handy 800m runner as a kid), but for some of the others it was hellish. Kevin Beattie was a terrible runner. He was fit enough and smart enough to be in the right place at the right time on a football field, but his forte was explosive speed and he struggled to run more than a couple of hundred metres at a time.

Midway through the 1978/79 season, Bobby had offered to double my wages to £110 a week. I didn't have an agent to advise me, but I found his offer a bit insulting and turned it down. That might sound odd, but I knew that others were on a lot more. Bobby reminded me that I'd be out of contract at the end of the season and there might not be another offer. But I said to him, 'Fine. But I found that yard of pace you wanted me to find in America and I feel great. I will become a regular in your first team and I will score goals.' It was a gamble and a bit cocky, but it paid off. Before the 1979/80 season began, Bobby offered me £300 a week and a £12,000 signing-on fee.

I went straight from signing that new contract to a

Toyota garage on the outskirts of Ipswich, where I agreed to buy a brand-new green Celica, which cost six grand but was one of the most beautiful things I'd ever laid eyes on. I'm not normally one to shilly-shally, but I told them I'd go away and think about it. So I jumped on the bus back into town and dropped by the bakery where we used to go for a coffee and a sandwich after training. When I walked in, Russell Osman was sat there having a cup of tea and reading a newspaper.

Despite coming through the youth system with Russell, I always got the impression he thought he was a wee bit above me, at least in the early days. I see Russell quite a bit now and he's as good as gold, but because he went to grammar school and captained England under-16s at rugby he always seemed a bit posh to a kid from Glasgow. He also used to hang about with the older lads, like Mariner and Mick Mills, while I was in the bookies or at the races with Gatesy and Paul Cooper. Anyway, on this occasion Russell said to me, 'What are you smiling at?' I very excitedly told him that I'd just signed a new deal and agreed to buy a new car, and he very calmly replied, 'Well done you. I've taken the plunge as well.'

'What, you've bought a new car?'

'No. A new house.'

I couldn't get my head around what he'd told me. He'd completely outdone me and dowsed my excitement. On top of that, someone as young as Russell shelling out for a house was as difficult to fathom as wormholes. He'd only just turned twenty, and who bought themselves a house at that age?

Once I'd lifted my jaw off the floor, Russell patiently explained that the house cost £24,000, but he'd put down six grand and borrowed the rest. Then he took me up to the estate to have a look around. As luck would have it, the place next door to Russell was still for sale. So I got straight on to the estate agent and put down a deposit before heading back to my digs, phoning the garage and cancelling the Celica. I bought myself a second-hand Triumph Dolomite instead. Good job I did, because whenever Butch had given his buddy Russell a lift to training, they'd never bothered knocking me up.

We had a poor start to the 1979/80 season but began to move through the gears as the months rolled by. By December we were almost unstoppable. After losing 4-1 to Coventry on 30 November, we didn't lose in the league until the final game of the season. We beat West Brom, Manchester City and Everton 4-0, but the highlight was a 6-0 hammering of Manchester United in March. United were vying with Liverpool for the title (which they hadn't won since 1967) and had a very good side, including Gordon McQueen, Steve Coppell and Ray Wilkins. But their manager Dave Sexton made the mistake of moving McQueen out to mark Gatesy in the hole, and Gatesy ran rings around him. I scored two, Mariner got a hat-trick and Thijssen netted the other one. It could have been far worse for United, because goalkeeper Gary Bailey saved three first-half penalties. Yes, you read that correctly. We eventually finished third behind Liverpool and United, which in those days meant we qualified for the UEFA Cup again. But we knew we could do better. In fact, I was certain we were good enough to be champions.

That summer, some of the boys went off to Hungary to film *Escape to Victory*. I think Bobby Robson knew the actress Anjelica Huston, whose father John was directing and was looking for professional footballers for his prisoner-of-war side (although a couple of the lads ended up playing Nazis). I'm always being asked why I'm not in it, and it's because I was playing for Scotland. I made my debut in Poland in May 1980 before playing Hungary a few days later. After the game in Budapest I met up with the Ipswich boys – Wark, Osman, Beattie, Cooper, Kevin O'Callaghan, Robin Turner and Laurie Sivell – at their hotel and was asked if I wanted to be involved, but I decided against it. The season had only just finished, I'd been with Scotland for a couple of weeks and I just wanted to go home and chill out. As it turned out, Huston made them work bloody hard. But I must admit, every Christmas when I see it on TV I think, 'I wish I'd stuck around.'

I'm told that Pelé's overhead kick only took one take, while Sylvester Stallone wanted it written into the script that he scored the winning goal, despite the fact he was the keeper. Russell actually got a couple of lines, probably because he was a good-looking lad, but Johnny Wark's only line was dubbed over, because they couldn't understand his Scottish accent. If you watch the film, you'll notice that Johnny is on the pitch one minute and sitting on the bench the next. That's because the team they played was a proper Hungarian league outfit and

Johnny got clobbered and had to go off. When he got back to Ipswich, he had to miss the first couple of weeks of pre-season.

Bobby Robson was a brilliant manager but not the cuddly uncle some people think he was. Bobby was from humble mining stock in Durham and could be tough. He certainly wouldn't hesitate to have a row with you, don't worry about that. But he wasn't a bastard for no reason and as long as you were performing on the pitch, he'd tolerate you socializing off it.

The defunct airline Pan Am used to sponsor a football tournament called the Sunshine International Series in Florida, and one summer it involved us, the Tampa Bay Rowdies, the Fort Lauderdale Strikers and São Paulo FC. We were in the departure lounge at Heathrow, having a couple of beers, when Bobby strolled over and said, 'Right boys, put those drinks down. You're not going over there to make a Hollywood movie. And you're not going to be lying on the beach all day, so forget your Ambre Solaire. This is the start of pre-season, so you're going to work your bollocks off and win the tournament.'

There was a bit of grumbling as we piled on the plane, but I was soon smiling again after discovering that we were in first class and my seat was right at the front. As soon as I sat down, an air hostess asked if I wanted a glass of champagne, to which the answer was a firm yes. By the time we were flying over Ireland, there was no champagne left on the plane. Bobby obviously got wind of this and had us working so hard on the beach the following morning that people were throwing up and all sorts. But the minute we got back to the hotel, we hit the poolside and got straight on the Budweiser.

We didn't really stop drinking for two weeks, but it didn't seem to affect our form. We hammered Fort Lauderdale and Tampa Bay to set up a final against São Paulo, who were staying in the same hotel as us. Their coach couldn't understand how we were managing to perform, because we were coming in at all hours of the morning and his lads were being good. São Paulo ended up beating us 1-0, but we absolutely battered them. We hit the post twice, hit the bar, and their goalkeeper had a blinder. After the game, Bobby said, 'Don't think I don't know what you've been getting up to.' But he was really pleased, because all that mattered to him was that we performed.

What Bobby wouldn't tolerate was anyone besmirching Ipswich's reputation. Another summer, we played in a pre-season tournament in Holland. After the last game they put on some food in the training camp and it was horrible. They'd also only laid on a few beers, so once they were finished we got stuck into the duty-free, which mainly consisted of bottles of advocaat. On one of the tables was a big pile of custard rolls, which weren't particularly pleasant either. So someone threw one at Butch, and things quickly got out of control. There was custard and advocaat everywhere and there were plates flying across the room like frisbees. It was complete mayhem, and the place got trashed. When Bobby found out, he went mad. We were supposed to travel home on the ferry first class, but he took our tickets off us and made us sit with the regular punters. I didn't mind because there was a casino in economy.

It's certainly true that Bobby sometimes left himself open to mockery. After a game against Sunderland, nearly a 300-mile drive from Ipswich, he told us to be on the bus by 5.15 and that anyone who wasn't on time would be left behind. All the players made it, but when it got to 5.15 Bobby was still chatting to fans by the players' entrance. So someone told the driver to leave. I'm not sure if he knew Bobby was on board or not, but he promptly closed the doors, started the engine and pulled away. We were all hiding down the back but could see Bobby running after us, shouting and waving his arms about. If that wasn't funny enough, Bobby suddenly pulled up, having twanged a calf muscle. While he was hopping about on one leg, we were literally rolling around in the aisle. I'm not sure I've ever laughed so much. By the same token, I'm not sure I'd ever seen Bobby so angry. When the club secretary David Rose finally got the driver to stop, Bobby clambered on board and let rip. 'Whose idea was that? Was it supposed to be funny?' Poor old David got a terrible bollocking, as did the driver. And while Bobby was being seen to by the physio, the players were desperately trying to get their breath back while wiping floods of tears from their cheeks.

Despite our successes on the field, we were never anything like celebrities. Back then, even Manchester

United players used to be able to drink in their local pretty much hassle-free. A lot of the locals knew who we were, but you have to remember that we were hardly ever on TV. We might appear briefly on *Match of the Day*, and we occasionally played live on ITV on a Sunday afternoon, but there wasn't the same blanket coverage that there is today. Gatesy was lucky because every time he scored a cracker, the cameras seemed to be there. But a lot of our goals weren't captured for posterity.

Ten of Ipswich's first team were internationals, but we didn't have any bigheads. We were all on decent money and able to live well, and when we were winning games I'd feel on top of the world. Sometimes, that meant I could be a bit lairy – luckily, there were no camera phones, so no one could take a picture of me with a pint in my hand and post it on social media – but something would always bring me back down to earth with a bump.

Despite earning decent money, top footballers in my day weren't what you'd call rich. We certainly weren't on a par with wealthy businessmen or people who worked in the City. Sometimes after a game a local businessman called Charlie Manning, who was born in a Gypsy caravan, built himself up from nothing and ended up owning half of Felixstowe seafront, would lend us his big black Bentley to mess around in. Nowadays, teenage footballers drive Bentleys worth £250,000. Back then, a Bentley was the stuff of a madman's dreams. We'd find a driver, and Mariner would normally play the role of rich tycoon, sitting in the passenger seat with his dark glasses on. And when the dream was over, I'd have to go back to my eight-year-old Dolomite.

Ipswich Town Football Club was controlled by the Cobbold family, who had their fingers in a lot of pies in Suffolk, including the Tolly Cobbold brewery. John and Patrick Cobbold were the grandsons of the 9th Duke of Devonshire and the sons of John Cobbold, who took over Ipswich Town in 1936, and his wife Lady Blanche Katherine Cavendish, who was the sister-in-law of British prime minister Harold Macmillan and English football's first female president. Lady Blanche was a real eccentric and a regular in the crowd at Portman Road. In 1955, the Cobbolds hired Alf Ramsey, who transformed Ipswich from lower-league strugglers into Division One champions in 1962, before leading England to World Cup glory in 1966. When John Jr stepped down as chairman in 1976 after developing cancer, Patrick took over. John and Patrick (known to all and sundry as 'Mr John' and 'Mr Patrick') were lovely guys, but proper eccentrics like their mother, and almost always pissed. Every time they saw me, they'd say, 'Aah, it's Alan Brazil. How are we, you stupid Scottish prick?' And I'd reply, 'Oh, hello, Mr John/Mr Patrick. Pissed again, are we?'

Ask anyone who played for Ipswich during their time in charge and they will have a story to tell about them. When Ipswich won the FA Youth Cup for the first time in 1973, the Cobbolds put on a big party for the families at a local hotel. They'd put a lot of money into the academy, so were absolutely thrilled. And at one point in the evening, John stood on a chair and shouted, 'I want every mum and dad here to get very drunk before going to bed and having more fun, because I want our kids to win the cup again in eighteen years' time!'

The Cobbolds surrounded themselves with various other Suffolk businessmen and landowners, all of whom were on the board. There was a Scottish farmer called Willie Kerr, who was a lovely old boy and whose son John took over as chairman when Mr Patrick stepped down in 1991; there was the seed merchant Murray 'Never in a Hurry' Sangster; there was estate agent and club director Harold Smith, whom everyone called Captain Pugwash. They were a real mix of characters, but one thing they had in common was that they all loved getting hammered, especially during Ipswich's various forays into Europe. After we played Saint-Etienne in the quarter-finals of the UEFA Cup in March 1981, we heard stories about all these upper-crust old English gentlemen being thrown out of a Michelin star restaurant in Lyon for being unruly. European cities were used to dealing with English hooligans by that time, just not hooligans as posh as the Cobbolds and their mates.

When Bobby Robson joined Ipswich in 1969, he got off to a dreadful start and fans were soon calling for his head. After yet another defeat during the 1970/71 season, Bobby was summoned to the brewery and feared the worst. But instead of sacking him, Mr John apologized for the fans' behaviour and gave him a rise. John was also responsible for the quote 'The only crisis at Ipswich Town is when we run out of wine in the boardroom.' Either the Cobbolds had more patience than modern owners or they were too pissed to notice how bad the team were. But keeping faith paid off spectacularly. Between 1972/73 and 1981/82, Ipswich finished outside the top six only once, were twice runners-up in the First Division, and won the FA and UEFA Cups.

We started the 1980/81 season in fine fettle, winning seven and drawing one of our first eight games, before getting a valuable 1-1 draw at Anfield. We didn't lose until November, when bottom-of-the-table Brighton beat us 1-0 at a freezing Goldstone Ground. But December was another good month for us. We managed another 1-1 draw against Liverpool, beat local rivals Norwich and drew away against Arsenal on successive days, meaning we finished the year one point behind Liverpool and Aston Villa with two games in hand. Johnny Wark was scoring goals from all angles, I was also chipping in with plenty (including one against Norwich, which almost took the roof off Portman Road), and we looked every bit like that season's champions. On top of that, we'd advanced to the last eight of the UEFA Cup. Me and the lads felt unstoppable, and Bobby now had so much faith in me that he shelved plans to buy a back-up striker.

The first two months of 1981 couldn't have gone much better. We won seven out of eight in the league, as well as our first three FA Cup ties, and were two points ahead of Villa and eight points ahead of Liverpool at the top of the table. At the start of March we beat European champions Nottingham Forest to advance to the last four of the FA Cup and Saint-Etienne to reach the semi-finals of the UEFA Cup, including a magnificent 4-1 victory over Michel Platini's men in the first leg in France. But towards the end of March, the wheels began to fall off. In the space of a month we lost five league games out of seven and an FA Cup semi-final against Manchester City at Villa Park.

Back then, the FA Cup was a far bigger deal than it is now and that defeat against City was probably the most devastating of my career. Growing up, it was my dream to play in a Scottish Cup final at Hampden Park, but playing in an FA Cup final at Wembley would have been almost as good. I still beat myself up over the chance I missed early in the game. Arnold Mühren centred and I tried to get my foot over the ball to hit it on the half-volley. But the ball died in a patch of sand and I completely miskicked it (always blame the pitch!). We were all over City that day but couldn't convert any chances. Kevin Beattie had a header cleared off the line, I had another opportunity, and so did Gatesy. And in extra-time, City's Paul Power scored with a free-kick. Had we won we would have beaten Spurs in the final because that Wembley pitch (with no patches of sand) would have suited us down to the ground.

A couple of days later we returned to the same ground to play Villa, a game that was hyped as the title decider. The morning after the FA Cup semi-final I'd woken up with a sore groin. But because we were staying in Birmingham for both games I wasn't able to get any treatment back at Portman Road. So I asked Villa's physio if he'd be able to help, and remarkably he said yes. On the morning of the game I arrived at Villa Park ridiculously early, so as not to get the physio into any trouble, and he cured me. A few hours later I scored the opening goal and we ended up winning 2-1. As I was walking off the pitch, the physio shook his head and gave me a look that said, 'Don't you dare say anything.' He thought he'd just handed us the title.

But the Villa physio need not have fretted, because wear and tear would be our ultimate undoing. Modern players and managers are always complaining about having to play too many games, but they have no real grounds for complaint. Premier League footballers play on perfect pitches with hardly any tackling. They're also aided by sports science, whereas we had to make do with rubdowns and a bucket and sponge. Squads were also far smaller in those days, which meant it was a lot more difficult to sustain challenges on different fronts.

By early January, Villa only had the league to worry about because they weren't in Europe and had been knocked out of both domestic cups. We'd knocked them out in the third round of the FA Cup, with Mariner finishing off a brilliant move that involved most of the team, but that was a bad result in hindsight. It meant that Villa were able to keep their first team relatively fresh, while our star players were going down like flies. Beattie only played seven league games, Burley was out for a long stretch, Thijssen had a spell on the sidelines, and Johnny Wark and I had bouts of flu. And while

Bobby had some decent reserve-team players to call on, they weren't really in the same class.

We managed to scrape a win against Manchester City, which meant we were four points behind Villa with a game in hand, but with only two games to play. If Villa lost to Arsenal and we beat Middlesbrough, a victory over Southampton would have landed us the title. Arsenal did indeed beat Villa at Highbury, only for us to lose up at Ayresome Park. Mariner scored to give us the lead at half-time, but Middlesbrough's Yugoslavian striker Bozo Jankovic netted twice after the break. Bozo is a hero to Villa fans to this day. We then lost our final league game of the season against Southampton, to finish four points behind champions Villa.

Not that I'm making excuses, but we played sixty-six competitive games that season to Villa's forty-six. Russell Osman made sixty-eight appearances in total, including two for England, while I made fifty-eight. If our squad had been bigger, we would have won the title that year. Villa were obviously a very good side – they went on to win the European Cup the following year – but we beat them three times that season, home and away in the league and in the FA Cup, and nothing will convince me that we weren't a better team.

Of course, we still had the UEFA Cup final to look forward to. We'd got there courtesy of a victory over FC Cologne. Cologne were full of German internationals, including goalkeeper Harald Schumacher, Rainer Bonhof and Pierre Littbarski, the last two past and future World Cup winners. They also had Tony Woodcock, formerly of Nottingham Forest, up front. They were a very good team who had won the Bundesliga a couple of seasons earlier, so a couple of our lads decided a bit of intimidation was needed.

Before the first leg at Portman Road, I remember Butcher and Mariner screaming and shouting in the tunnel and the Germans not knowing what to make of it. And Mariner could have been sent off after about three minutes. From an Ipswich corner, he smashed an elbow into the face of his marker Gerd Strack, before landing on his ankle. Strack was left semi-conscious and bleeding from the nose. Fortunately, the referee didn't see it and Johnny Wark went on to score the only goal, his twelfth of the tournament. In the return leg, Terry Butcher scored the only goal, a thumping header in the second half, and our place in the final, against Holland's AZ Alkmaar, was assured.

The first leg of the final was on 6 May, four days after our defeat at Middlesbrough, so Bobby had plenty of work to do to pick us back up. But he was always very good before those big occasions. He used to say, 'You can't let the fans down. They're the people who pay your wages and this game will be the highlight of their week. Put on a show so that they renew their season ticket.' Several of our team played that first leg at Portman Road despite carrying injuries: Thijssen had a groin strain, Mariner had a problem with his Achilles, Gatesy had only just recovered from a calf strain, and Paul Cooper had to wear a protective cover on his arm. But we managed to find a performance from somewhere and smashed Alkmaar 3-0, with goals from Wark, Thijssen and Mariner.

A three-goal lead should have settled the nerves, but a strange incident before the second leg in Holland a fortnight later left me very unsettled. Me and a few of the other lads were in the lift in the hotel when it suddenly ground to a halt between floors. We were stuck in that lift for about an hour, and when they finally got it moving again and wrenched the doors open, they found us all stripped to our underwear, because the heat was unbearable. On the way to the stadium I had a feeling that we weren't going to have it all our own way.

When Thijssen scored after just three minutes we led the tie by four goals and looked home and hosed. But we were running on fumes. At half-time, AZ were leading the leg 3-2. It could have been worse, because Paul Cooper had to make a couple of brilliant saves. AZ made it 4-2 on the night with seventeen minutes to play, but we managed to hold on to win 5-4 on aggregate.

The relief was immense. After a season in which we could have won the First Division and the FA Cup, at least we had a European trophy in the cabinet. When we returned to Ipswich and the locals came out in their thousands to cheer our open-top bus parade in the pouring rain, all the failures were forgotten. I was only twenty-one, so surely FA Cups and league titles would follow.

The following season we got off to a decent start in the league, winning five and drawing two of our first seven games, including victories over Manchester United and Liverpool in successive games (I scored the winner at Old Trafford and celebrated gleefully in front of the Stretford End). But we were knocked out of the UEFA Cup in the first round, by an Aberdeen side managed by a thirty-nine-year-old called Alex Ferguson – he whose front garden I'd desecrated a decade earlier. I was also struggling with a trapped nerve in my foot. Whenever I put it down, it was like stepping on a live cable, and I was having to get it jabbed before games.

After an operation to remove a growth on the nerve, followed by a miraculously quick recovery, Bobby Robson was saying to me in training, 'Wow. You look fantastic, son.'

'I'm ready to play.'

'Well, we've got a game on Tuesday night. Are you sure you're ready?'

'Absolutely.'

After training on the Tuesday morning, which was just a bit of five-a-side, Bobby came over to me and said, 'You look sharp as a tack. Well done you. Really looking forward to tonight.' So I thought I was definitely in the side.

The game was against Leeds in the League Cup at Elland Road, and I got to the ground early because I was so excited to be playing so soon after an operation. About an hour before the match, I was sitting in the changing room with my number 10 shirt on, screwing my studs in, when the rest of the lads started drifting in. Apparently, they'd come straight from a team meeting.

One by one they looked at the back of my shirt and started laughing. Then Bobby walked in and named the side, and I was only substitute.

I was absolutely livid. I pulled my shirt off, threw it on the ground, and everyone fell about laughing. But I didn't find it at all amusing. I told Bobby to get stuffed, that I wasn't playing sub, and stormed off to the shower. When Bobby's assistant Bobby Ferguson came and dragged me out, I thought it had been a wind-up and put my shirt back on. But when Bobby confirmed that I was indeed on the bench, I pulled my shirt off and stormed off again. That happened three times, until Bobby roared, 'Brazil! Get back in here and get that number 13 shirt on!' I did as I was told but spent the entire game sulking in the dugout.

Bobby Ferguson was as hard as nails, like a stereotypical sergeant major. I never liked him because he was a bully. Whereas Bobby Robson would take a struggling player aside and say, 'Come on, lad, give me twenty minutes after training and we'll put it right,' Ferguson would just shout at people. I recall a midweek away game against Stoke when the rain was coming down horizontally (the weather was always terrible at Stoke). A few of the lads had had a little bet, because we thought we'd hammer them. But having gone 1-0 down, we were hanging on for dear life. When things weren't going great, Ferguson would scream directions from the touchline. On this occasion he told me to move to the wing so that Gatesy could play alongside Mariner. I could see Ferguson out of the corner of my eye, foaming at the mouth and waving his fist. But because I was on a scoring streak, I wouldn't budge. Ferguson shouted to Gatesy, 'Tell your fucking mate to get out here on the left!' When Gatesy tried to pass the message on, I blanked him as well. Eventually, Mick Mills played a ball down the line, right in front of the dugout, and when I went to fetch it, Ferguson grabbed me by the throat and told me where to go – literally.

Ferguson's tactical instructions didn't work out, because Stoke scored a second. Afterwards, while Ferguson was ranting and raving in the dressing room, I took my gear off and wandered down to the communal bath. Ferguson followed me, still screaming his head off, and in the end I stood up in the bath, put my fingers in my ears and said, 'I'm not listening to you any more, you're a prick.' With that, Ferguson started pulling his gear off. I thought, 'Here we go, we're going to have a fight in the bath . . .' Behind Ferguson I could see loads of faces peering around the door – Cooper, Gatesy, Mariner – and just as he was about to wade into the bath, a couple of the lads grabbed hold of him and dragged him away. At the time I was more worried about the money I'd lost on the bet. But that incident was the beginning of the end of my time at Ipswich.

Rumours had been circulating for months that the boss might be moving on. Even before the UEFA Cup final, Sunderland had offered him a deal worth £1 million over ten years, which was silly money in those days. And now he was being linked to the England job. Bobby was becoming less involved in team affairs, leaving a lot of the nitty-gritty stuff to Ferguson. And we didn't get on. On top of that, the club was spending a lot of money on upgrading the West Stand, which meant that players were probably going to have to be sold.

It was around that time that I put in a transfer request. Bobby Robson wasn't in that day, so I handed it to the chairman, Patrick Cobbold. That evening, Bobby phoned me and tried to talk me out of it. He told me I'd acted on impulse, that he wished I'd spoken to him before writing the transfer request, that I was a key member of his team and that I wasn't going anywhere. I loved the city and didn't want to uproot my wife Jill, who was from the area and surrounded by family. I'd even been considering bringing my mum and dad down from Scotland. But despite Bobby's kind words, I had no intention of withdrawing my transfer request. The bottom line was, I didn't feel loved by the club and thought other clubs might appreciate me more.

Bobby picked me for the game against Manchester City in November, which was the start of a nine-game winning streak. But in February 1982 we were well and truly put in our place by Liverpool. In the first leg of our League Cup semi-final at Portman Road I was asked to play on the left again. I gave it my best shot but just didn't feel comfortable, and Liverpool beat us 2-0. Four days later we played them again in the league at Anfield and I was dropped for the first time in my career. I was devastated and resentful, and we lost 4-0. I was picked for the second leg of the League Cup semi-final and managed to find the net, but we could only manage a

2-2 draw. And a few days after that we were dumped out of the FA Cup by Second Division Shrewsbury at Gay Meadow.

What we didn't need at that precise moment was a game against the league leaders. Southampton had only lost one of their previous thirteen games and hadn't been beaten away from home since October. They had some proper players, including Kevin Keegan, Mick Channon, Dave Watson and Alan Ball, and I didn't really fancy our chances, not least because Paul Mariner was injured.

I spent the afternoon of the game in the bookies. I'd taken an early price on a horse and it was running in one of the last races at Newmarket. To make things worse, there was a stewards' inquiry that went on for about twenty minutes. I waited and waited and eventually the right result came in. I grabbed my winnings, jumped in the car and drove as fast as I could to Portman Road. The money was handy, but it wasn't ideal preparation for a big game.

There were rumblings of discontent in the changing room before the game, but when we got out on the pitch, all our worries disappeared. I scored a hat-trick in five first-half minutes and added two more after the break. In case you've lost count, that adds up to all five of my team's goals in a 5-2 victory. I'd never even scored a league hat-trick, and now I'd become the first Ipswich player to score a league nap hand. Going into that match, things were looking a bit grim for both me and the team. But that was one of the greatest nights of my life.

It just goes to show: you never know what's around the corner.

I've got two match balls at home, because the ball I scored the first four goals with got booted out of the ground. Having grabbed the second ball, the local newspaper put out an appeal, asking for the first ball to be handed in. It was the sort of thing they write when someone's pet dog goes missing. A couple of days later, a guy who worked in Churchman's cigarette factory behind the ground turned it over. The story goes that the guy's son was future Ipswich and England goalkeeper Richard Wright.

Four days later we went to Leeds and I scored perhaps my best-ever goal in a 2-0 win. I received the ball about 40 yards from goal, noticed the keeper was off his line, and lobbed him. Unfortunately there were no cameras at the game – just as there were no cameras at the Southampton game – so you'll just have to take my word for it. That goal, and my effusive celebration, made me a bit of a pantomime villain to Leeds fans. When I moved to Manchester United a few years later, they hated me even more.

After I retired, I was invited to watch Leeds play Arsenal at Highbury. We were having a few drinks in a box and the Leeds fans were making an almighty racket, so I wandered outside with a glass of wine in my hand to take a look. Below me were hundreds of Leeds fans with their tops off, singing 'Marching On Together'. Suddenly, one of them spotted me and started chanting, 'He's bald, he's fat, he talks a load of crap, Alan Brazil!'

They all turned around and joined in, and while they were singing this little ditty, they missed their team scoring down the other end. I thought that was hilarious. But the next thing I knew, two coppers came in, told me I was in danger of inciting a riot and locked the door to the balcony. I had to watch the rest of the game on TV. Then in 2018 I was voted the most hated man in Leeds, just because I'd never heard of their new manager Marcelo Bielsa.

After a bit of a stumble in February and March we got on a real roll, winning ten and losing only one of our next fourteen games. Unfortunately, Liverpool were on an even better run. Having been only mid-table at Christmas, they won eighteen of their next twenty games. And when we lost our penultimate game of the season at Nottingham Forest and Liverpool beat Spurs on the same afternoon, the title was theirs. For the second season running, we were the bridesmaids.

Despite being Ipswich's top scorer that season with twenty-eight league goals, I wasn't sure I'd be at the club for much longer. In July 1982, Bobby Robson replaced Ron Greenwood as England manager, as had been expected. The Cobbolds had offered him an improved ten-year deal to stay, but Bobby was a patriotic man and was never going to say no when his country came calling. What was worse, Ferguson was named as his replacement, Bobby having recommended him to the board.

Because of the new stand, we knew Ferguson had no

money to strengthen the squad, and when Arnold Mühren joined Manchester United (on a free transfer) and Paul Cooper and Eric Gates also put in transfer requests, I started getting twitchy. We didn't win any of our first six league games and were beaten by Roma in the first round of the UEFA Cup. As early as September journalists were questioning the wisdom of appointing Ferguson as manager, and Patrick Cobbold was forced to defend him. But the writing was on the wall. As one reporter wrote, 'They sold a team to build a stand.' Bobby's departure certainly didn't help, but that was pretty much the gist of things.

When I put in another transfer request, this time it was accepted. I'd already got wind that Manchester United and Spurs were after me, as well as West Brom. The idea of linking up with Mühren again at Old Trafford particularly appealed to me. But Ipswich were asking for £800,000, which seemed a bit unrealistic.

In January 1983 we were scheduled to play Charlton in the third round of the FA Cup. Whenever we played in London or on the south coast, rather than travel from my home in Stratford St Mary to Portman Road, my wife would drop me at a bus stop on the A12 and the team bus would pick me up from there. But on this freezing cold winter's morning, the rendezvous time came and went. After another fifteen minutes ticked by, a supporters' bus pulled up and someone jumped out and said, 'We're going to the game, want a lift?' I told them that the team bus was picking me up and must have been delayed. But twenty minutes later I was still standing there, shivering my bollocks off.

Eventually, my wife happened to drive past on her way to the shops. She told me she'd been past Portman Road and the bus had gone. I couldn't believe it. I was thinking, 'It's the FA Cup and they've left me behind, all because I want to leave the club.' I got in my wife's car and told her to step on it, because I knew the team would be stopping off at the Post House Hotel in Brentwood. But when we pulled into the car park, the team bus was nowhere to be seen. When I went inside, the receptionist told me that it had left fifteen minutes earlier. I jumped back in the car and told my wife to head into London.

I wasn't sure where Charlton's ground was – in fact I didn't even know it was south of the River Thames – but when we got to Tower Bridge, a car with a Charlton scarf hanging from the window pulled up alongside us. I wound down the window and said to the driver, 'Are you going to the Valley?'

'Yeah,' he replied. 'Aren't you supposed to be playing?'

'I might not be unless you help me.'

Luckily, they took mercy on me and offered me a lift. Poor Jill had to turn around and head back to Ipswich.

When I ran into the dressing room, everyone was glaring at me and I ended up having an almighty row with Ferguson. He claimed the bus had come to pick me up from my house, to which I pointed out that it had always picked me up from the bus stop. Although he didn't put it to me directly, I later learned that Ferguson thought I was trying to get out of the game to avoid being cup-tied when I joined a new club. If that was the case, why did I bother getting my wife to drive all the way to London?

As it happened, I played against Charlton, and we won 3-2. But a few weeks later Ferguson told me to play a midweek game for the reserves, which triggered another argument. Ferguson suggested I wasn't trying, which was an outrageous accusation. Every time I pulled on a football shirt, whichever team I was playing for, I gave it everything I had.

Fans are always making similar accusations about players, but it's rarely a case of players not trying. Instead, they're probably just lacking in confidence, not getting the ball where they want it, and getting a bit disheartened as a result. If it's your job to run around a lot, chase lost causes, harry, tackle and give the ball to people who can play, it's a lot easier to mask that feeling. But a player who needs the ball to show how good he is can appear disinterested, even when he's not. It's just not in their nature to go looking for the ball; it's not what they're trained to do.

Take Arsenal's Mesut Özil, whom people are always calling lazy. He's a great talent, but Arsenal clearly aren't getting the best out of him, especially away from home, where he has a tendency to drift in and out of games. But I don't think it's because he's lazy, it's because his confidence is shot. I said to ex-Arsenal midfielder Ray

Parlour many a time, 'If I was Özil's manager, I'd put my arm around him and say, "Look, son, I know you're not a tackler. But do a bit more chasing back when you can and demand the ball, because when you're on the ball, we're a better side."' That's all he needs, a bit of comfort from the boss. And that's all I needed from Ferguson. But I was never going to get it.

After being relegated to the reserves and accused of laziness, it dawned on me that rather than putting a ridiculously high price on me to deter suitors, they'd done it because they were desperate to raise money for the new stand. Mick Mills had been sold to Southampton in November 1982 and it was clear that others would soon be out of the door. Ipswich didn't have the money to put players' wages up and most could earn more money elsewhere.

Our league form had improved as the season wore on but in February we were knocked out of the FA Cup by our arch rivals Norwich. A couple of weeks later I scored in a 3-1 victory over Birmingham. That was my last goal for Ipswich. The following week we were thumped 4-1 by West Brom. When we got back to Portman Road, Ferguson told me that the club had accepted an offer. I assumed it had come from Manchester United, but it had come from Spurs.

As I've said, my wife was from Suffolk and I'd only just managed to persuade my parents to move down from Glasgow, after years of trying. But I didn't have much choice. The following day I met Spurs manager Keith Burkinshaw at a hotel in Braintree, Essex. There was no agent involved, it was just me, Keith and another club official. We had a cup of tea, discussed terms, and shook on the deal in less than an hour. It was a four-year contract, paying better money than Ipswich. On the way home I stopped at a phone box and told Jill to start looking for houses in London. That's how fast it happened.

3

Losing It

I didn't want to leave Portman Road, but it was something I had to do for my career. I needed a new challenge and had no reason to believe I wouldn't be as successful at Spurs as I had been at Ipswich. Keith Burkinshaw assured me during our brief meeting in Braintree that he was going to build the team around me. But that left me under a lot of pressure, because Spurs had paid almost £500,000 for me, which was a lot of money in those days. And because the squad was bigger than Ipswich's, the battle for a place in the starting line-up was more fierce. At Ipswich, as long as you performed on Saturday, you could take it a bit easy in training. But at Spurs, training was like a cup final every day.

For a while, things worked out. I scored six goals in twelve games at the end of that 1982/83 season, including one in a 5-0 victory over Arsenal, which endeared me to the fans, and two in a 3-1 victory over Ipswich, which felt really weird. Those guys hadn't just been team-mates, they'd been great pals. And still were. I'd known Terry Butcher and Russell Osman since I was a kid, and now I was being marked by them. The old pride kicks in when that happens, and you want to do your best. But I wouldn't call it an enjoyable experience. I certainly didn't celebrate, even though those goals helped Spurs qualify for the UEFA Cup.

But there were worrying signs amid the goals. In my fourth game I was substituted midway through the second half, having never been substituted at Ipswich. As far as I was concerned, being substituted meant the manager thought you weren't good enough. And after I'd calmed down, I had to admit I hadn't played well.

Off the pitch, things looked rosy. My wife had found us a lovely house in Hertfordshire and my first daughter Michelle was born in August 1983. But on the pitch, something wasn't quite right. During the 1983/84 pre-season I didn't feel sharp and seemed to have lost that yard of pace I'd found in Detroit. My back felt uncomfortable and I couldn't help noticing that I wasn't as fit as I used to be. Despite the nagging doubts, I remained determined to succeed at my new club. And at that stage, I genuinely thought I would be successful.

Spurs had some great players. There was Ossie Ardiles, who was a tremendous athlete and very clever. He could just run and run and always wanted to bring other players into the game with little one-twos and wall passes. Ossie's fellow World Cup-winning Argentine Ricky Villa was more of an individual talent, but still an excellent player. We had a brilliant, vastly experienced goalkeeper in Ray Clemence, a couple of tough centre-backs in Paul Miller and Graham Roberts, Chris Hughton at full-back, Micky Hazard in midfield, alongside the skipper Steve Perryman, who was always barking orders, and a few top strikers in Steve Archibald, Garth Crooks and Mark Falco. The only guy I was never quite sure about was our Irish winger Tony Galvin. He was a great player, always bombing up and down the wing, but he never smiled. He had a degree in Russian and I'm sure he was a Communist. When he joined us down the pub, he used to sip half a bitter and tell us all off for being too flash.

Then there was Glenn Hoddle, who had also just signed a new contract. Glenn was a quiet guy, but a great character. He loved his music and had a penchant for the Eagles. He was also a wonderful player with a real swagger. He always looked in control, except maybe against top teams like Liverpool, who would get stuck into him and put him off his game. He had a beautiful touch and could do unbelievable things with the ball, with either foot.

Like all great players, Glenn was always thinking one step ahead and seemed to know exactly where his team-mates were, even before he got the ball. If I set off on a run, I could be almost certain that Glenn would find me, just as Arnold Mühren had always been able to find me at Ipswich. Sometimes, Glenn would play the perfect through ball and I'd have to apologize for not reacting. It was always my fault, not his. With Glenn in your team, you always thought you had a chance. And as a striker, you always believed he would provide you with plenty of ammunition. No wonder the fans adored him.

Despite being surrounded by all that talent, I still hadn't scored a goal six games into the 1983/84 season.

On top of that, we lost 3-1 to Ipswich on the opening day. That game was at Portman Road, which felt really strange again. The Ipswich fans weren't nasty, as today's fans often are to players who have left. But even though there weren't many players left from my time there, it still felt like going home, and not in a good way. In truth, Ipswich never stopped being 'my' club.

Against Nottingham Forest in October, which was shown live on ITV, I was substituted again. A few days after that we were playing Lincoln City in the Milk Cup, which I thought would be the perfect opportunity to grab a couple of goals and boost my confidence. But I wasn't even picked for the squad. Instead, I had to watch the game from the stands. And the following day I was told to play for the reserves. I didn't mind playing for the reserves when I was coming back from injury, but to be dropped there when I was trying as hard as I could to make things work was a bitter pill to swallow.

The manager said he thought I was lacking in confidence. He was right. I was still only twenty-four, but suddenly my belief had gone. However, that happens a lot with players when they join a new club. Good managers don't wash their hands of them, they have faith and try to make things right. But my relationship with Burkinshaw was deteriorating fast. Keith was a quiet man who let his assistant Peter Shreeves do most of the day-to-day stuff and let the players get on with things. And that was no good for me. I needed a boss who was going to put his arm around me and tell me how good he thought I was.

It was around this time that I started hearing that Manchester United and Everton were interested in signing me. That was exactly what I needed to hear. If two of the biggest clubs in the country wanted me, I couldn't be as bad a player as Burkinshaw seemed to think I was. And even though I'd signed a four-year contract at Spurs, I wouldn't have been able to live with myself if I'd spent all that time on the periphery of the first team.

When I discovered that Burkinshaw had turned down the advances of United and Everton, I was furious. Burkinshaw was now telling the press that he couldn't sell me because I was such an important member of his squad, despite the fact that he wasn't picking me. Between the start of the season and Christmas, I played in only a handful of games. And when I did play, I didn't play very well. I was banging in the goals for the reserves, but that wasn't going to do it for me. So I handed in a transfer request. For whatever reason, Burkinshaw then picked me for an away game against Notts County, in which I played well. Then in March 1984 I scored in both legs of Spurs' UEFA Cup quarter-final victory over Austria Vienna. But I was dropped for the semi-final against Hajduk Split, despite scoring four goals in five games in Spurs' run to the last four.

A few weeks before the end of the season we were playing against Queens Park Rangers. After going two goals down, and with hardly any time left on the clock, Burkinshaw said to me, 'I suppose we'd better put you on.' I should have just done as I was told, but my pride was dented. I wasn't going to be spoken to like that, and

I was hardly going to score a hat-trick in three minutes. So I told him exactly what I thought of him and refused to go on. Looking back, we were both frustrated. He wanted the player he'd bought from Ipswich for so much money, while I just wanted him to show some belief in me. Alas, I wasn't even in the eighteen-man squad that travelled to Brussels for the UEFA Cup final against Anderlecht; I watched it from my living room in Hertfordshire. I got a winners' medal, but not to be involved in the final hurt.

The previous June I'd played for Spurs against Manchester United in an end-of-season game in Swaziland. I'd mixed with the United lads and played particularly well, which was one of the reasons United's manager Ron Atkinson was so keen on signing me. Burkinshaw left Spurs at the end of the 1983/84 season, but when United came in for me, I was relieved beyond belief. That Atkinson had persuaded his board to pay £700,000 for me suggested that I was still a decent player with a lot to offer. I'd been in and out of the Spurs team, and I couldn't help thinking that the move would reinvigorate me.

After I'd put pen to paper, the Spurs lads gave me a great send-off at Royal Ascot. We went down in three Rolls-Royces, had a great day, and rounded off the festivities at the Elephant on the River, just down the road from the MI5 building on the Thames. The last thing I remember about that evening was taking Glenn Hoddle home to Old Harlow and having to almost carry him through his front door. It was hard to leave those Spurs boys behind, but when Manchester United come calling, you can't really say no.

Unfortunately, my stint at United was less successful than my stint at Spurs. United's medical people didn't notice anything wrong with me, just as Spurs' medical people hadn't, but however hard I trained, I just couldn't recapture the fitness I'd had in my Ipswich days. And that just made me pine even more for Portman Road. I was substituted in my first game at Old Trafford, against Watford, and the fans soon got on my back.

I managed to put a good run together after that, scoring five goals in seven games, before twisting my ankle. When I finally recovered from that, I couldn't get back into the team. The competition was fierce, as I was battling for a place with Mark Hughes, Frank Stapleton and Peter Davenport. And by the beginning of 1985 I had lost Atkinson's backing and was playing for the reserves. I played the occasional first-team game over the next few months, but it was quite clear that my future lay elsewhere.

The night before the FA Cup final that year against Everton, me and my room-mate Bryan Robson were watching a preview on ITV when the presenter Dickie Davies announced our team. That's how I discovered I hadn't made the twelve, despite scoring twice in a 3-1 win against QPR the previous week. I was absolutely gutted. I didn't like being on the bench, but I would have made an exception for an FA Cup final. Norman Whiteside scored that classic winner in extra-time as

United won the trophy for the sixth time, but I barely celebrated on the train back to Manchester – that's how bad things were.

When you go to a massive club like United, you've got to perform week in, week out, otherwise they won't put up with you. In football, players are just pieces of meat, completely expendable. I understand that, because it's a business. But that didn't make it any easier. When I signed for United, just as when I signed for Spurs, I thought I'd score in every game. But I'd lost 15 per cent without knowing why, which was incredibly frustrating. Not only had my fitness and pace dropped off, I also wasn't as powerful as I'd been. The medical people thought it might be down to problems with my hamstrings or groin, but couldn't be more specific than that. Nowadays an MRI scan would have picked up the problem, but there were no MRI scans back then.

Not that my United team-mates were anything but supportive, and I became particularly good pals with my skipper Bryan Robson. Our daughters were about the same age, and we'd take them swimming at the Mere Golf Resort and Spa in Knutsford. One Sunday our wives took the girls home and we stayed on for a few frames of snooker and a couple of pints. Later, Trevor Francis turned up. He was playing for Sampdoria at the time but was over for a few days and staying with Bryan in Hale. I was always bumping into Trevor during my football career. I'd played with him in America and we'd had some great battles when I was playing for Ipswich and he was playing for Nottingham Forest.

Anyway, when Trevor turned up at the golf club he was carrying a load of Italian knitwear, and that kind of gear was all the rage. So I bought a few jumpers from him, we had a few more frames of snooker, before Trevor said, 'We need to go, Bryan. Dinner's on.' So I offered to give them a lift home in my new Granada, which I was rather chuffed with. Trevor jumped in the front, Bryan jumped in the back, and off we went.

We were snaking along the back roads from Knutsford to Hale when I looked in the mirror and noticed that Bryan wasn't looking too well (apart from the very expensive Italian jumper he was wearing). He'd gone green and looked like he might throw up. I asked him if he was OK, he said yes, so I carried on. But a couple of miles later, Bryan started making sounds like he was going to be sick. Trevor was going mad – 'Bryan, you're the England captain!' – and Bryan was telling him to shut up. To be fair, I don't think he'd drunk too much, I think it was the combination of new car smell and winding roads. Anyway, I pulled over and Robbo jumped out and disappeared into the woods. We could hear him vomiting and I thought it was hilarious, but Trevor wasn't amused and was tutting away next to me, like he was Bryan's mum.

Once he'd done what he had to do, Bryan got back in the car and I carried on driving. About a minute later, Trevor started shouting, 'Stop! Stop! Stop! Bryan, where's your jumper?' It turned out Bryan had been sick down the front of it, taken it off and thrown it in the woods. Trevor went mad and insisted we go back and find it. I said to him, 'Trev, it's just a jumper,' and he replied, 'It's not just a jumper, it cost about £200!' After a bit of an argument I turned the car round, and when we got back to the spot where Bryan had jettisoned his jumper, Trevor started telling Bryan to look for it. Bryan was having none of it, and even offered to pay Trevor double, and eventually Trevor got out of the car and flounced off into the woods.

I was pissing myself, but by now it was quite dark and Bryan wanted to get home. So he said to me, 'Just leave him, Al.'

'But he's in the woods.'

'Just go, he'll find his way home.'

'We can't! We're in the middle of nowhere.'

Suddenly we heard Trevor shouting, 'I've found it!', before he emerged from the darkness holding this jumper out in front of him. I told him to stick it in the boot and off we went.

Whenever I think of that scene it tickles me: Bryan Robson, Captain Marvel, being sick over his £200 jumper and Trevor Francis, Britain's first £1 million footballer, desperately searching for it in a dark wood halfway between Knutsford and Hale. You couldn't make that stuff up.

My relationship with Atkinson having disintegrated to almost nothing, I became training-ground fodder during the 1985/86 season and was often asked to make up a defensive wall when we were practising set pieces. That wasn't what I'd dreamed about when I was a bright-eyed kid growing up in Glasgow. My team-mates were great, but the fans hated me. I was constantly booed, and one fan even spat at me. Atkinson never spat at me, but there were times when I thought he might. He'd spent £700,000 on me and I hadn't lived up to his expectations.

One week, Atkinson ordered me to play for the 'A' team against a bunch of kids in Stoke. Another time, I went to see the band Sad Café in Manchester (appropriately, their biggest hit was 'Every Day Hurts'), and the following morning my wife woke me up to tell me that Ron had been in touch and I had to go in for a trial game, even though it was supposed to be my day off. I played for the reserves against the first team and banged in three goals, only to be left out of the squad for that weekend's match. Eventually, Ron lost his rag and told me, in no uncertain terms, that I had no future at the club, unless I wanted to rot in the reserves. I didn't know why he was so angry with me, because I was trying my hardest, but I had no choice but to go somewhere else.

Coventry City came in for me and I played for them until the end of 1985/86, but things didn't get any better. In one game, against Ipswich, Cyrille Regis, God bless him, played a ball through and Terry Butcher beat me to it. I thought, 'What the hell's wrong with me? There's no way Butch should be faster than me.' He certainly never used to be. I didn't last long at Coventry, and was offloaded to Queens Park Rangers in the Second Division.

By now my back was in agony after every game. That's if they could get me on to the field in the first place. I'd get up in the morning and have to wash and brush my teeth with one hand on the sink, because I couldn't support the weight of my head while bending forward. If I took my hand off the sink, my head would crash into the porcelain. That's when I really knew I was in trouble and started to think my career might be over. QPR were great about it, sending me to specialists and paying for therapy, but nothing worked.

In the end, I took things into my own hands. I visited an acupuncturist in Newport, had injections in my groin and hamstring in St John's Wood, and, as a last resort, travelled to a seaside town in Essex to see a mad doctor who was supposed to have cured the great ice hockey player Wayne Gretzky. Someone had told me this doctor had a 'special' injection that would tighten the muscles at the base of my back and hold things in place. I thought this sounded fantastic, so I drove down the following morning. When I turned up at this doctor's beautiful pink cottage, he wasn't there. A nurse led me into his surgery, told me to lie on the table, and I remember being really excited, thinking that I was about to be administered with a miracle cure. Every time I heard a car, I'd run to the window, because I thought my saviour had arrived.

Eventually, the door opened and this ancient guy shuffled in. He was bent double with his arms behind his back. He was like a cross between Groucho Marx and Igor from those old Frankenstein movies. Not what I'd expected.

Groucho told me to take my shirt off and turn over.

Now there was no escape. He had me where he wanted me, and I'd just have to grin and bear it. When he started rubbing my lower back, the pain caused my head to shoot up, so that I could now see the doctor in a mirror. I watched in horror as Groucho produced a giant syringe full of dark fluid from behind his back – like something you'd buy in a joke shop – before pinning me down by the back of my legs. While I was thrashing around on the table and cursing my head off, I swear to God he said to me, 'Do not be alarmed, Mr Brazil, this treatment has proved effective for many species.'

What did he think I was, a talking horse?

Groucho didn't just insert the needle, release the murky fluid and take it out again. Instead, he inserted the needle and moved it around, so that I could feel it scraping against the flesh inside me. It was absolutely excruciating. Between my screams and swearing, Groucho told me that he was moving the needle from ligament to ligament, and this went on for so long that my screams eventually turned to dry retching. Then, suddenly, he said, 'Mr Brazil, stay there for twenty minutes, you'll be fine,' and off he shuffled. I did as I was told and remember thinking, 'If this treatment is so effective, why doesn't the doubled-up old bastard use it on himself?'

I never saw Groucho again, and while his treatment might have worked on many species, it certainly didn't work on me.

In January 1987 I visited a rather more conventional specialist, who told me my spine had degenerated, so that the bottom disc was shot away. He advised me to stop playing football and that I could do permanent damage if I tried to carry on. There was some talk of having a spinal fusion, but that was a very dangerous operation in the 1980s. So I took the doctor's advice and quit. In a strange way I was relieved, because at least I knew what was wrong with me. But it was a hammer blow nevertheless. The overriding sensation was fear. I was only twenty-seven and suddenly unable to do the only thing I'd ever wanted to do. I also had a wife and daughter to look after. How was I going to provide for them now?

4

Pride of Scotland

As a kid, if I wasn't dreaming about scoring the winner for Celtic against Rangers in a cup final at Hampden Park, I was dreaming about scoring the winner against England at Wembley. And if not against England at Wembley, then against Brazil in a World Cup. Because then, unlike now, Scotland playing on the biggest stage was entirely normal, almost expected.

Despite its meagre population, Scotland has produced some of the greatest players in the world: Rangers midfield colossus Jim Baxter, Leeds dynamo Billy Bremner, Manchester United legend Denis Law, Lisbon Lion Jimmy Johnstone – the man almost every young Celtic fan wanted to be in the playground – Celtic and Liverpool great Kenny Dalglish, more of whom later. Things ain't what they used to be, but I'll return to that a little later too.

The story goes that shortly after my five goals against Southampton in February 1982, Saints manager Lawrie McMenemy bumped into Jock Stein at a function and wouldn't stop going on about my performance. And having not played for Scotland since winning those two caps in Eastern Europe in 1980, I was picked for a friendly against Spain at the end of that month. If it wasn't for Lawrie, a proud Englishman who would one day become England's assistant manager, I might never have played for Scotland at the 1982 World Cup.

Being picked for that tournament was an incredibly gratifying moment, especially as I was the youngest player in what I regarded as one of the strongest Scottish squads ever assembled. I mean, just look at the players who went to Spain that summer: my hero Kenny Dalglish, one of the greatest British players of all time; his Liverpool team-mates Alan Hansen and Graeme Souness; my Ipswich team-mate Johnny Wark, who was one of the most potent midfielders in Europe at the time; John Robertson, who had won two European Cups with Nottingham Forest. Every man in that squad was a key player in either a top Scottish or English team and twelve of us had won European trophies. That wasn't a great squad in hindsight, like some people think, it was a great squad *then*.

Dalglish made his Celtic debut when he was just seventeen, so I was watching him from when I was a wee boy. By the time I moved to Ipswich, Kenny was a massive star and almost certainly the best player in Britain. He had this great knack of knowing which foot to take the ball with and shielding it with his arse, so that the defender had to come all the way around him. A lot of the time he wouldn't need to take a touch, because he knew exactly where his team-mates were before he received the ball and always seemed to have two or three options in his head. And that was just his build-up play. Anywhere in and around the box, he was magic at spinning defenders and curling goals in. And when he got half a yard clear of a defender, he wouldn't necessarily smash it because he had other finishes in his locker, including that little dink over the keeper. But Kenny wasn't all about vision and skills. He also kept himself in great shape, wasn't afraid to tell a team-mate off if he wasn't doing his job properly, and was a terrific whinger, constantly in the referee's ear.

Some Celtic fans never forgave Kenny for joining Liverpool in 1977. You have to remember that Scottish club football was a lot stronger back then and Celtic had won the European Cup only ten years earlier. As far as those fans were concerned, Celtic was the biggest club in the world. But Kenny made the right decision to head south, because he won six league titles and three European Cups with Liverpool and is probably their greatest ever player.

Amazingly, a lot of non-Celtic Scotland fans didn't take to Kenny to begin with, but they didn't have a choice in the end because he scored some absolute crackers on the international stage. I'd put him in the very highest bracket, along with players like Pelé, Maradona, Cruyff, Best, Messi and Ronaldo. He really was that good.

When Souness, in his role as a Sky pundit, criticized Paul Pogba's performances for Manchester United, Pogba claimed he'd never heard of him. That's fair enough, because Pogba wasn't even born when Graeme retired. But those of us who played with and against Graeme will never forget the experience and understand why he finds Pogba's attitude so baffling. Graeme was the perfect pro. He trained like a demon, didn't mess about, and knew exactly what his job was on the pitch. He could snap you in half with his tackling, score goals, was an excellent passer and a great leader of men. Even off the pitch he was immaculate. He was always smart and knew when to rest and when to loosen his collar and have a couple of drinks.

That Liverpool team he played in was full of great players, but there was only one person in charge. Unlike Pogba, when things were going wrong, Graeme didn't go missing. Instead, he did everything in his power to try to turn things around for his team. In that respect he was similar to Steven Gerrard and Roy Keane, great players of a more recent vintage. And when the skipper is doing that, it inspires team-mates to do the same. All in all, Graeme was the kind of player who made you think, 'I wish I was a bit more like him.'

One thing Kenny and Graeme couldn't do was sing. I only mention this because even before the squad was picked we had to perform our World Cup song, 'We Have A Dream', on *Top of the Pops*. That was a strange old day. Jock Stein wasn't very happy about the whole thing, because he regarded it as a distraction. And we weren't the only football team on the show that day. The England squad were also there, spouting a load of nonsense probably, as well as the Tottenham squad, singing their FA Cup final song with Chas & Dave. God knows what the other acts thought. In those days, being asked to appear on *Top of the Pops* was every pop star's dream, and they ended up sharing a stage with a bunch of footballers instead of Duran Duran or Spandau Ballet.

The producers made the mistake of having us rehearse

last, which meant we spent the whole day in the BBC bar. By the time it got to 7.30, we were all absolutely hammered. If I remember rightly, Depeche Mode were also on the show, although I don't remember seeing them in the bar. Tight Fit were also there, as well as Bananarama and Fun Boy Three. We came on after Patrice Rushen singing 'Forget Me Nots'. What Patrice made of the whole thing is anyone's guess. Firstly, she was American, so probably didn't know what football was. Secondly, she was an accomplished musician and was nominated for a Grammy that year. 'We Have A Dream' wasn't. But we certainly put in the most enthusiastic performance of the night. I remember the producer telling us to sway in the background, behind the actor John Gordon Sinclair (star of the hit film *Gregory's Girl*) and BA Robertson, who wrote the song. After ten pints, we didn't really need telling.

Our pre-World Cup training camp was in Portugal, where we acclimatized to the heat, played golf and a lot of cards. Nowadays you're always hearing stories about players being bored at major tournaments, but that wasn't the case with me. I was a twenty-two-year-old about to play in a World Cup and mingling with heroes – what did I have to be bored about? We didn't have any internet, there was only Spanish TV, we only had one phone call home a week and we certainly weren't allowed to drink. But there were a lot of characters in that group, including some very funny guys like John Robertson, Gordon Strachan and Dalglish. People often thought Kenny was a bit dour because he was very guarded with the press, but when he was in the company of people he trusted, he was a typical Glasgow boy and you couldn't shut him up. He was very dry and very witty and could cut you down with a single quip.

But it wasn't all sweetness and light in that squad. I'd played with some of the Scottish-based guys in youth football, people like Celtic's Roy Aitken, and was too young to be involved in any political stuff, so everyone welcomed me with open arms. But there was certainly a little bit of animosity between the English- and Scottish-based players. During the 1982 Home Championship, all the Scottish-based players would be sat around one table, the 'Anglos' would be sat around another and the coaching staff would be sat around another. It was natural to an extent, because Dalglish, Souness and Hansen played for Liverpool, while me, Johnny Wark and George Burley played for Ipswich, so we were mates. But there was a bit more to it than that.

However, with Jock Stein in charge, those splits were never going to become a problem. And no one was going to misbehave. Every time Jock saw Strachan outside, he told him off, because Gordon was almost transparent and Jock thought the sun was going to kill him. But the only player who got into proper trouble was Souness, because he kept sunbathing when Jock had told him not to. I think that was Jock sending a message to the rest of the group: 'If I can give the captain of the great Liverpool team a bollocking, none of you are safe.'

We were also kept entertained by Scottish fans, who came to Portugal en masse and would follow us whenever we left the hotel complex, including around the golf course. We'd find them in the trees when a drive went awry. And when we moved our base camp to Sotogrande in southern Spain, the fans multiplied by about a thousand. But Jock made sure they were kept at bay, while also throwing in a bit of entertainment to break up the monotony.

After training one day, Jock said he had a surprise for us. We piled on the bus, headed off on this mystery tour and stopped at a beautiful villa near Marbella with a massive Scotland flag outside. Rod Stewart soon emerged, wearing the skimpiest of tartan swimming shorts, before inviting us all in. We had a great afternoon, chatting about football and music. Rod was one of my biggest heroes and I'd seen him in concert a few times. A photo of that day has pride of place in my flat in London: me, Rod, Asa Hartford, John Robertson and Alex McLeish wrapped in a St Andrew's flag on the stairwell of the bus.

The opening game of our group was the USSR against tournament favourites Brazil in Seville, which we all went to watch. The Soviets, who were actually a pretty decent side with Dynamo Kiev legend Oleg Blokhin up front, were leading with fifteen minutes to play, before Socrates equalized with a ripper from long range and Eder bent in a left-footed winner with two minutes to go. In those days most Brazilians played for clubs in their home country, so seeing them for the first time was both a revelation and quite intimidating.

I was picked for our first game, against New Zealand in Málaga, which I was naturally overjoyed about, not least because it was on my twenty-third birthday. But things didn't turn out as planned, at least for me. Because our food intake was restricted in Portugal and I was burning up a lot of nervous energy, I lost loads of weight. And while we knew it was going to be hot in Spain in June, we didn't anticipate it being the hottest Mediterranean summer for twenty-five years. The temperature in the Estadio la Rosaleda was over 100 degrees and when I walked on to the pitch it felt like someone was holding a hot iron about an inch from my face. It was far from ideal for a pasty-faced lad from Glasgow.

I kicked off the match with my hero 'King' Kenny, which was a dream come true and one of my proudest moments in football. But I was jittery, which normally meant I didn't play my natural game. We got off to a flying start, Gordon Strachan setting up Kenny for our first goal after a storming run and Johnny Wark adding two more before the break, with me setting up his first. The ground seemed to be almost all Scotland fans and was absolutely rocking. They were the Tartan Army to most people, but we'd started calling them the 'San Miguellians', because they always had cans of San Miguel in their hands. There were people swinging shirts around their heads, banging drums and even playing bagpipes, although I have no idea how they got them past security.

Unfortunately, the temperature stubbornly refused to drop, even though we'd kicked off at 9 p.m., and I struggled to keep pace with the action. I was in pieces in the changing room at half-time, sweating buckets and seeing double. When Jock asked if I was OK to continue, I just nodded. I couldn't speak because my tongue was stuck to the roof of my mouth. And when we re-emerged for the second half, it seemed to be even hotter.

Jock's instructions were to play it safe and conserve our energy for our second game against Brazil three days later. But that was easier said than done. I was taken off after only eight minutes of the second half because my legs had turned to fag ash and I was now seeing treble. And when New Zealand scored two quick goals to make it 3-2, I was lying on a bench on the touchline, wondering where I was. I was eventually led to the changing room, and about twenty minutes later Strachan staggered through the door. He looked like he'd been stranded in a desert for a month, and I don't think it was any coincidence that the two fairest-haired lads in the team suffered the most in those conditions.

Thankfully, we scored two late goals to make things safe, John Robertson netting with a peach of a free-kick and Steve Archibald heading in from a corner. I was still lying down when the lads trudged back into the changing room, followed by two men in suits. I thought they were doctors, come to give me some treatment, but they were actually dope testers. They handed me a bottle to pee in, but I couldn't manage it, because I was so dehydrated. I drank pints and pints of water before my physio told me that drinking too much might cause my brain to swell. I tried orange juice and a couple of beers, which usually did the trick, but that didn't work either. After about five hours they told me to go back to the hotel and come back the next day. But the following morning they told me not to bother. I did get weighed, though, and I discovered I'd lost 10lb. No wonder my shorts were falling down and my boots felt like a frogman's flippers when I was finally substituted.

Despite our big win over the Kiwis there was frustration in the camp that we'd let them score those two goals, fearing that they might come back to haunt us. And it soon became clear that I wasn't going to be fit for the game against Brazil in Seville, against a side that had lost only twice in thirty-four games. The dehydration and dramatic weight loss had made me too weak even to train, so Archibald was picked instead of me. I'd have to watch the likes of Zico and Socrates from the stands rather than share a pitch with them.

Seville was even more humid than Málaga and I remember watching the teams singing the anthems from behind the dugout: our lads were all red-faced and sweaty from their warm-up while the Brazilians looked fresh as daisies. We were going along quite nicely for the first eighteen minutes before full-back David Narey went and bent one in from 35 yards. Why did he do that? What a fool! It was the footballing equivalent of knocking Muhammad Ali down in the first round.

David's stunning goal, the only one he ever scored for Scotland, woke Brazil up and they proceeded to murder us. Those Brazilians weren't just technically brilliant, they were also big, physical and mobile. Zico equalized with a free-kick before the break and they scored three more in the second half to make it 4-1, including a sweet lob by Eder over our goalkeeper Alan Rough.

To reach the second round, we now had to beat the

Soviets back in Málaga, because they had a better goal difference than ours (a legacy of the two soft goals we conceded against New Zealand). I felt strong enough to play, but Jock disagreed and started with Archibald, Robertson and Joe Jordan up front, with me on the bench. To this day I honestly don't know why Dalglish wasn't even a substitute for that game. Maybe there had been a falling-out or he had a niggle, but the fact that there wasn't a big thing made of it shows you just how respected Jock was: he was the big man, the first British manager to win the European Cup, so no one questioned him, not even the press. Besides, Archibald, who was good into feet, and Jordan, who had a lot of hustle and bustle and was with AC Milan at the time, were both very good strikers.

It was Joe who put us ahead after eighteen minutes and we continued to batter them until they equalized after the break. Jock stuck me on with about twenty minutes remaining and I had a couple of chances, but a horrendous mix-up between Alan Hansen and Willie Miller allowed the Soviets to take the lead with six minutes left on the clock. Souness made it 2-2 a couple of minutes later, but it was too little, too late, and we were eliminated.

If I had a pound for every time I've been asked why Scotland didn't do better in Spain, given the squad we had, I'd be a very rich man. The second round for that tournament consisted of another group stage, this time four groups of three teams, the winner of each group going straight into the semi-finals. The USSR were in with Poland and Belgium, and to this day I think that if we'd beaten the Soviets in that first round of group matches, we would have made the semis. And after that, who knows?

The San Miguellians were magnificent that night, even though we felt we'd let them down. Scotland fans are the best in the world, there's no doubt about it. Irish fans are similar, but they're not as good as the Scots. The locals love them, because they spend a lot of money on food and booze, love a sing-song, and don't smash the place up. Tournament organizers, TV people and neutral fans also love them because they bring so much colour to an event. It's a crying shame they've missed so many tournaments over the last twenty years.

The changing room after the game was like a morgue and we traipsed on to the bus in near silence. Because of all the Scotland fans wanting to get a sight of us, the bus took about an hour to get out of the ground. In those days there was no motorway between Málaga and Sotogrande, so we had to take a winding coastal road instead. And in every town we went through there were Scotland fans banging on the bus, singing songs and waving scarves, as if we'd won the World Cup. I felt like saying to them, 'You lot do know that we're out of the tournament?' That was one of the most incredible journeys I ever made.

My original plan was to have a couple of quiet drinks at the hotel, but by the time we saw the signs for Marbella, the fans' celebratory mood had started to rub off on us. Some of the players' friends and families were out in Puerto Banus, not far from Marbella, none of us had had a bevvy for weeks, and John Robertson was dying for a fag. So we got Graeme Souness to ask the boss if we could join them for a 'few drinks'. This wasn't a given, because Jock was a teetotaller as well as a disciplinarian. When Graeme came back, he shrugged his shoulders and said, 'He's going to think about it. He'll be down in a minute.'

We were halfway through Marbella old town when Jock made his way down the back and launched into a stirring speech: 'It's heartbreaking we couldn't have beaten those Russians and gone through. But you've all been a credit to each other, your families, your clubs and your country.' This was all very nice, but you could see that everyone was thinking the same thing: 'Can we go and get leathered?' And then Jock said: 'I'm going to ask the driver to pull over when we get to Puerto Banus. If anyone thinks they need a few drinks to get over the disappointment, I won't hold it against them. In fact, I won't even know. I will look the other way as you're getting off the bus. Just remember, you are ambassadors for your country, so behave with dignity.'

As the bus continued along the Golden Mile, Kenny Dalglish was shaking his head and saying gravely, 'Don't do it, lads. Don't do it . . .' Gordon Strachan was telling everyone we'd never play for Scotland again if we did. Eventually, we heard the indicator ticking and the bus pulled over. Puerto Banus was a magnificent sight, a seething mass of San Miguellians against a backdrop of twinkling boats and yachts. And within seconds, the bus was surrounded. It reminded me of the victory parade after Ipswich won the UEFA Cup. But this was ten times as manic, and we hadn't actually won anything.

Eventually, Jock shouted, 'If anyone wants to get off, I'll look out of the window and count to three.'

No one moved. Another few agonizing seconds passed, until Frank Gray shot up and grabbed his bag from the luggage rack, which triggered a stampede to the front of the bus. People were literally climbing over each other to reach the door. About thirty seconds later, the bus pulled away with only Jock and a few others on board. I couldn't tell if Jock was still looking in the other direction, and I didn't really care by that stage.

Bouncers bundled us into a bar called Sinatra's and a magical night ensued. Despite their best efforts, the bouncers couldn't stop us being mobbed by over-excited San Miguellians and most of the squad were soon without their tracksuit tops. Jock had told us to behave with dignity, but there wasn't a lot we could do about it. Some of us had changed into fresh Scotland shirts before leaving the stadium, and they were soon ripped off our backs as well. Someone even nicked my tracksuit bottoms and I had to borrow a pair of shorts to protect my modesty. Things got even more surreal when a huge cheer went up and Rod Stewart entered the building. Rod slung his arms around me and Alan Hansen and together we sang 'Sailing' while standing on the bar.

I awoke on a pedalo at 4 a.m. Rod was nowhere to be seen and I felt worse than I'd ever felt in my life. The only saving grace was that the pedalo was parked on the beach and not floating out at sea. Having found my bearings, I fell into a taxi, headed back to the hotel and managed to make it back to my room without being spotted by Jock.

The fact that that was my main concern, given the state I was in, shows you how much we feared him.

When I awoke at midday, the hotel was desolate. Davie Provan was dozing by the pool, as was his wont, and Alex McLeish was sitting in the bar nursing a black coffee. Between grunts and groans, Alex was just about able to inform me that the rest of the lads had headed back to Puerto Banus and were partying on a boat owned by a pal of Dalglish's. That sounded like a bit of me.

By the time I arrived, the party boat had long since set sail. But instead of heading back to the hotel and dozing by the pool with Davie or drinking coffee with Alex, I decided to make the most of my last day in Spain. When I walked back into Sinatra's, I was greeted like a conquering hero. And when I bumped into an old journalist friend of mine from Ipswich, the Bacardi and Cokes suddenly started going down smoothly.

In modern football, journalists and players are rarely friends. But in my day, that was quite normal. Steve Curry from the *Daily Express* was great. I could tell him anything and he wouldn't stitch me up. The *Sun*'s Alex Montgomery was also a good guy, as were the *Mirror*'s Jack Steggles and Steve Stammers, who worked for a few Fleet Street newspapers and sadly passed away recently. When I was playing in Europe with Ipswich we'd have half of Fleet Street on the plane with us. They'd all be down the front getting pissed with the Cobbolds, then Bobby would let them down the back to have a few drinks with the players. Bobby would say to them, 'If you stitch any of them up, you won't speak to them again.' They hardly ever did. In those days, football journalists were good at keeping secrets.

Nowadays, the relationship between players and journalists is shot through with suspicion. If you can even call them relationships, that is. For a start, they've got nothing in common. Back in the seventies and eighties, some football writers would have been earning as much as some of the players; in today's game, a football writer will be lucky to be earning as much as the physio. We had great respect for some of those writers, whereas now the players regard them as a nuisance to be avoided at all costs. It doesn't help that the actual football journalists are repeatedly undermined by news hounds from the same publication. It doesn't matter if you weren't the journalist who stitched a player up; if the story was published in your newspaper, that player won't speak to you again.

I'm sure that was a memorable day in Puerto Banus with my old reporter buddy from Ipswich. I just can't remember much about it. I do recall waking up on the beach, surrounded by recently extinguished fires, before staggering off to find a taxi. That didn't go well, because none of the taxi drivers spoke English. I couldn't remember where the hotel was and I didn't have any money anyway. Eventually, and just when I was starting to panic, a kindly Brummie bar owner took pity on me and whisked me back to the hotel, where the lads were already boarding the bus. When I walked into my room, Johnny Wark was a mixture of anger and relief. Luckily, he'd already packed my bag for me. I had a quick shower and shave, climbed on the bus and closed my eyes. When I

arrived in London, via Glasgow, I was met by my wife
and dad. I was in such a state, I felt the need to make up
some nonsense about hitting turbulence over the Alps.
The smell coming off me said something different.

I assumed I'd be playing for Scotland at the next World
Cup, when I'd be better equipped for the biggest stage.
Alas, my international career unravelled before my club
career did and I only had a few more Scotland games
left in me.

I was in Jock's squad for the 1983 British Home
Championship, the annual tournament involving Scotland, England, Wales and Northern Ireland that had
been running for a hundred years. Because I still hadn't
scored for Scotland, Jock gave me pelters when I turned
up for the training camp: 'I see you scored another one
for Spurs, Brazil. When are you going to get one for
your country?' In the game against Wales at the end of
May I finally broke my duck in a 2-0 victory, which was
the first time we'd beaten the Welsh in Cardiff for years.

That game was on a Saturday, and the following Wednesday we were set to play England in the tournament
decider, on the same day as the Derby at Epsom. When
we got to our hotel in Harpenden, Jock said to us, 'Well
done, lads. Great result. Now we can go to Wembley
and beat the English.' And we really thought we would,
because ours, as I said, was a proper Scotland team.

Following training on Monday, Jock said to me, 'That
goal has done you the world of good. You look sharper,
more confident.'

'Thanks, boss.'

'Are you looking forward to Wednesday?'

'Yeah, can't wait, boss. England at Wembley, doesn't get any better.'

'No. I don't mean the game, I mean the Derby.'

'The Derby? Oh, yeah. Yes, boss, should be good.'

'A little bird tells me you've had a bet.'

One of the Liverpool boys had told him I'd backed a horse called Teenoso at 33-1, which was now the favourite. And I'd put something like £100 on it. Because Ipswich was so close to Newmarket I had spent a lot of time down there (much more of which later), and the year before the Derby in question, someone had said to me, 'We've got a lovely two-year-old who could win next year. You should back him now.' Teenoso was a decent horse but his odds had got even shorter after Lester Piggott, the 'housewives' favourite', decided he was going to ride him.

I didn't realize the boss was interested in racing, but it turned out he was a big gambler. So after training on Tuesday, he collared me again and said, 'Have you had a little think about your bet?'

'What bet?'

'In the Derby. The favourite.'

'Oh yeah.'

'I'll tell you what we'll do. I hear you got him at 33-1. Let me have a little bit of your bet at 20-1 and if the horse gets beat, you'll get your money back.'

'What? Nah, boss. He's 9-2 favourite now, he likes a bit of cut in the ground and the forecast is rain, so he's likely to come in even shorter.'

'Don't be greedy, Brazil . . .'

I left it at that, but that evening my room-mate Johnny Wark suddenly got all serious and said, 'When they say the boss loves a bet, he *really* loves a bet. You'd better think about what he said.'

On the morning of the match we were doing a little sharpener, just some five-a-sides and set pieces, when Jock wandered over and said, 'Have you thought any more about my offer?'

'Nah, boss, please leave it.'

'You're right, I was a bit out of order. What about I have a bit of your bet at 16s instead of 20s?'

'Please, boss. This horse is 9-2 favourite and it's going to rain!'

'12s? Last chance, Brazil.'

'Nah, I can't, boss. Seriously, I can't.'

Now the lads started winding me up like you wouldn't believe – 'Come on, you tight bastard; why don't you give the boss a bit of your bet?' – but I refused to buckle.

We still didn't know who was in the team for the England game, which was a bit weird. I'd just scored my first goal for Scotland, the boss had told me how sharp I looked and I was wondering what was going on. But Jock was obviously going to keep everyone guessing until just before kick-off.

After we'd finished the sharpener and had a bit of lunch, we were told to meet in the physio's room at three o'clock. The masseur was a guy called Jimmy Steele, who stuck pages from the *Sporting Life* all over his walls and always had the racing on the telly. The lads spent a lot of time in there, whether they needed a massage or not, because they'd place bets on Steeley's phone. So there we all were, waiting for the Derby to start, and I was rubbing my hands together because it was raining in Epsom. And just as they were pushing the last few horses into the stalls, the door opened and the boss walked in.

The first thing he said was, 'Where's Brazil?'

'Here, boss.'

'12-1, take it or leave it.'

Before I could answer, he added, 'Have you ever played at Wembley before, son?'

'No, boss, I haven't.'

'OK then. Last chance. Have I got the bet or not?'

'Sorry, boss. I can't do it.'

With that, the race got under way. The result was never really in doubt. Teenoso went out fast and was third at Tattenham Corner, before Piggott stepped on the accelerator and brought him home for a three-length victory. Teenoso earned me a fair few quid that day, over three grand. But when the boss announced the starting XI, there was one change from the team that beat Wales: despite having scored my first goal in Cardiff, I was dropped, for Charlie Nicholas.

I'd just moved to Tottenham and had the same car sponsor as my Spurs team-mate Graham Roberts, who was playing for England in that game. This car dealer, Eric, had said to Graham, 'If you score against the Jocks, you can have a Porsche.' And while I was sat on the bench, Graham hit an absolute screamer from about

35 yards out, missed by a couple of inches, and I burst out laughing.

Jock turned to me and said, 'What are you laughing at, Brazil?'

I came on as a substitute in the second half but never played for Scotland again.

5

Getting On With Life

Although my days as an elite sportsman were over, I managed to squeeze a few more years out of my football career. How I ended up playing football in Australia in 1988 is a very strange story. I was out in London one night and got chatting to a guy who said he was an ex-Yugoslavia international doing a bit of scouting for Australian teams. And after a few beers he asked if I fancied playing for a team called Wollongong. I had never heard of Wollongong, but when he told me it was near Sydney, I told him that sounded like a great idea.

I was only being polite, but a few days later my phone rang in the middle of the night. I thought something bad had happened, but it was actually a guy called Harry Michaels, who would go on to produce the *Aerobics Oz Style* television series and was at that time involved with Wollongong FC. Harry thanked me for agreeing to join and told me that visas were on their way for me, my wife and two kids (my second daughter Lucy had arrived in 1985). I thought I must have been dreaming, but a few weeks later we were all on a plane bound for Australia.

To be honest, I viewed it as more of a holiday, though I ended up playing against lots of Greeks, Italians and

Yugoslavs, and they all wanted to give the Pom a kicking. I was only supposed to play three games, but we won two and drew one and they asked me to stay on for one more game in Melbourne, which was where my brother lived at the time. We won that game as well, me and the family flew home, and then I got another call from Harry, telling me that they'd lost their latest game and needed me to come back. I ended up going back for six games, four of which we won and two of which we drew.

I flew home again, and the following week Wollongong's centre-forward broke his leg. So I went back for another eight games, and brought another player with me, a guy called 'Bruiser' Keyes, a roofer who had been on the books at Luton but was now plying his trade at non-league Bury St Edmunds.

Bruiser and I flew business class, which meant a lot of free champagne. The problem was, we were landing on the Saturday morning and playing that night. When we arrived at Sydney Airport, Harry was there to meet us, very excited. I had to tell him we'd had a terrible flight and needed to sleep, half of which was true. The match was the first soccer game at the new Sydney Football Stadium, against Sydney Olympic. About twenty minutes in, Bruiser beat two men on the wing, crossed, and I tapped in at the far post.

But what I remember most about that game is that I was just about to take a corner in the dying moments, and faffing about to waste as much time as possible because I was blowing out of my arse and Sydney were all over us, when someone in the crowd shouted, 'Pelé!' When I looked up, an old friend called Alec Jamieson was beaming back at me. Alec was a schoolboy international for Scotland and played with me for Ipswich's youth team before emigrating to Australia. He eventually got into chemicals, selling cleaning fluids and the like. I clambered over the wall, jumped into the crowd and gave him a big hug. And when I got back on the pitch, the referee gave me a yellow card for time-wasting. We did, however, hang on for the win.

After the game, all I wanted was my bed. But Harry was deliriously happy because he'd stuck a big bet on and won ten grand (apparently, he'd only bought Wollongong because Sydney Olympic didn't want his money, on account of him being a Greek Cypriot), and he insisted we go out on the town. We took Alec with us, had a huge night, and when I went into Alec's room the following morning, it was a wreck. Alec, who was obviously out of practice when it came to boozing, had been violently ill and the place smelled to high heaven. I went off and had a swim and a bit of breakfast, and when I returned to Alec's room it smelled like a pine forest, with notes of wild flowers and a summer breeze drifting through it. When Alec appeared, he was holding a leather bag aloft which contained his cleaning products. Alec smiled and said, 'Think of this bag as my American Express card – I don't leave home without it.'

I also ended up playing in Switzerland because of Trevor Francis. Trevor knew a guy called Raimondo Ponte, a former Nottingham Forest team-mate and

Swiss international who was then manager at FC Baden, who played in the Swiss second division. Trevor said to Raimondo, 'You've got to get Brazil over there; he'll do a job for you for a season.' So Raimondo did, and I had a ball.

My family came out with me and we were there for about a year. Baden is a medieval town just outside Zurich, with cobbled streets, beautiful little bistros and patisseries and a river flowing through it. We had a great time, including learning to ski, which led to my eldest two daughters skiing for their country as juniors. We trained every night, but it wasn't as intense as training back in England, which suited me.

The only problem was that the players over there didn't really drink. I eventually persuaded Raimondo to allow us to go out one night a week, but the first time there was a misunderstanding as to where we were supposed to meet. I was sitting in this bar with a guy called Arnaud, the first-team coach, and there was no one else to be seen. Fifteen minutes turned into half an hour and eventually I thought, 'Never mind, I might as well get stuck in anyway.'

The following morning, Arnaud didn't turn up to training. We were doing a bit of stretching when Raimondo wandered over and said, 'Alan, what happened last night?'

'Well, me and Arnaud ended up in one bar and the other lads must have gone to another. We had a great time though.'

'You had a great time?'

'Yeah. Why?'

'Because Arnaud hasn't turned up to training and I've spoken to his wife. She tells me that Arnaud was drinking with you for ten hours.'

'Oh.'

'And you can't speak German and Arnaud can't speak English.'

I told Raimondo that we communicated through the common language of Becks.

I scored quite a few goals for Baden, including a couple of hat-tricks, and played against some decent pros. One pre-season game was against Pisa, who were in Italy's Serie A at the time. They beat us comfortably and had a great English kid at the back who turned out to be Paul Elliott, who went on to play for Celtic and Chelsea. But in the end, even Raimondo's gentle training regime proved too much for me and we had to return to England.

Back home, I played a bit of non-league football in Essex, turning out for teams like Chelmsford City and Stambridge United. My brief spell as player-manager of Witham Town was interesting. Jimmy Greaves's son Danny was up front and on a fiver a goal. Knowing how greedy strikers are, I soon put a stop to that. One week we played local rivals Braintree in the cup, when they were managed by my old Ipswich team-mate Roger Osborne, who scored the winner in the 1978 FA Cup final. But instead of playing up front, I ended up playing in a three-man defence with two of the slowest full-backs in England. The regular centre-half got drunk the night before and couldn't get out of bed. Midway through the first half I told the two full-backs that I'd be better off defending on my own and sent them forward. The tactics worked a dream, because in the dying minutes I bent a free-kick into the top corner to win the game. I thought that had made me a bit of a hero in Witham, but we recently had one of my old Witham team-mates on the breakfast show, and he reckoned that most of our transfer budget went on keeping me in champagne.

They say that sportspeople die twice, first when their career comes to an end, and then when they shuffle off this mortal coil. A lot of footballers just don't know how to handle retirement. They blow all their dough, turn to drink, destroy relationships and their lives end up in ruins. Take Paul Gascoigne. That man was a genius, could do anything with a football, but he was like a nine-year-old in a man's body. Take the football away and he was lost, like a child without his mum. So many people have tried to help him, including old team-mates, old clubs and the Professional Footballers' Association (PFA). But the only thing he wants is to play football again, which no one can make happen.

Not long ago I did a gig with Gazza in London, and when I hugged him he was like a bag of bones. He was good that night, full of old stories, probably because he felt comfortable in the company of football fans who loved him. But I fear for him, because while people can keep helping him back to his feet, it's up to him to stay there. And how many times can a man come back from the brink? George Best was the same. I got to know George very well because we did *Soccer Saturday* together on Sky, and after the show was done we'd always have a couple of glasses of wine at Isleworth Rugby Club. But he didn't want to talk to anyone else, he just wanted to sit in the corner and have a quiet chat with me, Rodney Marsh and whoever else was on the show that day. That was sometimes awkward, because Rodney and I loved the company of strangers. If someone politely asked for George's autograph, he'd be polite back and sign his name. But if someone was pestering him, you could see him getting angry. Like Greta Garbo, he just wanted to be left alone. But because he was such a superstar and people loved him so much, that wasn't possible.

At that gig I did with Gazza, there was an ex-pro on each table. And on one of the tables at the front was former Arsenal and England full-back Kenny Sansom. After I'd finished interviewing Gazza, I noticed that Kenny had gone. I got talking to one of the people on his table and he told me that at some point during the interview Kenny had slid off his chair and disappeared under the table with a bottle of wine. I thought this guy must have been exaggerating, but when I lifted the tablecloth, Kenny was still under there. That was the first time I realized that Kenny had a major problem.

Recently, Ray Parlour and I were leaving the talk-SPORT car park at Blackfriars (before we moved to the new building at London Bridge) when I saw Kenny sitting in this small wood. I don't know if he'd slept the night there, but he was wearing a dirty old trench coat, had hair past his shoulders, a beard, and looked totally disorientated. I remembered Kenny as a smart, good-looking lad and now he looked like a tramp. Ray and I didn't know what to do. I was going to give him some money, but Ray told me not to, because he'd just spend it on more booze.

Because of his Arsenal connections, Ray knew a lot more about Kenny's situation than me. The PFA are based in the City, not far from Blackfriars, so we phoned them up and they agreed to send a car. Fifteen minutes later, this car turned up, they bundled Kenny in the back, and that was the last time I saw him. Apparently, Crystal Palace, another one of his old clubs, had been trying to look after him, but he'd spend every penny he earned on alcohol. Last I heard, Kenny was learning to walk and talk again after being beaten up in Exeter.

Seeing Kenny like that, a guy who won eighty-six caps for England and played in two World Cups, was a real slap in the face. And so many ex-footballers go the same way, including some you never in your wildest dreams thought would. I had no idea Ray Wilkins, Kenny's old England team-mate, had a serious drink problem until he was on the show and had to come off air because he was slurring his words. Afterwards, he said, 'Al, when I get the taste, I can't help myself. I pop into all the old boozers from when I was a player and end up blacking out.' I couldn't believe it. Working with Ray on the show was always a joy. He was always immaculately dressed, had a lovely manner about him, and was one of the nicest men you could ever wish to meet.

The first time I met Ray was in the late 1970s, when I was at Ipswich and Ray was at Chelsea. We were on our way to a game at Stamford Bridge when our bus got stuck in traffic on the King's Road. Bobby Robson ordered us to get changed into our kit and when we eventually got to Stamford Bridge we literally had to run directly from the bus to the pitch, bypassing the changing room completely. As you can imagine, the Chelsea players thought this was hilarious and were slaughtering us. All except for one, namely Ray Wilkins.

Chelsea had a huge amount of experience in that team – players like Ron 'Chopper' Harris, Kenny Swain, Micky Droy and Ian Britton – but Ray was the skipper, and had been since he was eighteen. He was an elegant player, with excellent awareness, and just as classy off the pitch. After the game, which we won 3-2 (Chelsea finished bottom of the table that season, 1978/79, and were relegated), Ray came up to me and said, 'Hello, pal. I just wanted to say you've got a great left foot.' He was genuinely interested in me, despite the plight of his team, and I never forgot that. And whenever he spoke about his time playing for Rangers, he was never condescending about Scottish football, like some English players are. He genuinely loved Glasgow and the Scottish people.

Whenever he was on the show, he'd make sure he was there an hour before it started and would buy coffee and breakfast for all the backroom guys. And when I finally rolled in at 5.55 and asked him how he was, he'd always reply, 'Dangerously well.' After one show, Ray said to me, 'What are you up to now, fella?' It was a beautiful sunny day, so I told him I was going to walk down to Borough Market and have a glass of champagne outside a great little bar I knew. Ray replied, 'I wish I could join you,' before bidding goodbye and heading off with his driver. I walked into this bar and was about to order a glass of champagne when the barman placed a bottle of Moët & Chandon in front of me. I said to him, 'Who's that from?' He replied, 'The guy behind you.' When I turned around, Ray was sitting in the corner grinning at me. He had one glass and said goodbye again. That's the guy I'll always remember.

When Ray died in 2018, my phone didn't stop ringing for days. That was because everyone in football loved the guy and was devastated at his passing. And when his son spoke about his struggles with depression and alcoholism at the funeral, it was like he was speaking about someone I'd never met.

People have a go at the PFA, saying they don't do enough to help players, but they only have so many staff and can't keep track of everyone. For every Paul Merson, who went through hell with drugs, drink, gambling and mental illness, but who was famous enough for people to reach, there are hundreds of men who played in the lower leagues who are lost to the system.

I love a drink, but I'm lucky in that I also know when enough is enough. And while I wasn't happy when I had to retire from football, it didn't break my heart and spirit in the way it does some people's. Unfortunately it's a very thin line and many people slip over the wrong side.

I can't help looking at people like Kenny, George and Gazza and thinking, 'There but for the grace of God go I.'

I knew a lot of people in the City, so I ended up selling insurance up there. I'd get the train there and back from Suffolk every day and I quite enjoyed it. But I didn't want to be stuck in an office for the rest of my working days, so I decided to buy a beautiful old pub in the heart of Ipswich called the Black Adder. Buying a pub was just what retired footballers used to do, and it was very successful in the early days, full of Ipswich fans. I'll never forget Ipswich playing Brighton on the last day of one season and beating them to avoid relegation. We almost ran out of beer before the game, that's how busy it was. And after the game there must have been five hundred people inside the pub and another thousand outside. They had to shut the road off, and we only closed when we ran out of alcohol. The pub was literally dry and it took us two days to restock.

They were great times, but once the media work had started up, I couldn't be there all the time. And when I was there, I'd stand behind the bar and everyone would want to have a drink with me. It got to the stage where I was permanently cream-crackered, living off booze and what wits I had left. I could never relax, because I was always worried there might be a bit of trouble. I didn't know anything about business, spent money on renovations and trusted people I shouldn't have. After eighteen months I started getting screwed by the creditors, especially the brewery, who were merciless. In the end I had to sell everything to pay off the debt the pub had accumulated. I wasn't the first former footballer to fail at being a landlord, and I'm sure I won't be the last.

My old talkSPORT sparring partner Mike Parry says to me, 'Nothing seems to bother you. If you went skint, you'd still be able to sleep at night.' He's right. When I lost the pub, instead of getting depressed I rolled my sleeves up and got on with life. I used to say, 'Things might be bad today, but tomorrow could bring untold fortunes.' People think I'm flash, but back then I was driving around in an old Morris Minor that Jill's dad had bought as a collector's item. We had to sell the house, which was a beautiful Georgian place in a nice part of Ipswich, and move into a much smaller place around the corner. I wouldn't call it the worst moment in my life, but I was really pissed off for my family.

I'll always remember saying to my oldest daughter, 'Don't worry, things will get better.' She told me not to worry and that she liked the new house, and I replied, 'I know it's a nice house but it's not as nice as the one we had. Mark my words, we won't be here long. And when we do move again, it will be to a better house than the one we had before.' That was my attitude to life: if I got knocked down, I was going to rebuild and come back even stronger.

6

Hirings and Firings

How I became a radio presenter is a strange and circuitous story. I'd done a few co-commentaries for BBC Radio Suffolk in the 1990s, as well as some bits and bobs on the telly. If there was a Champions League game on the Wednesday, I'd discuss it on the GMTV sofa the following morning. That meant driving all the way from Ipswich to London, parking the car and getting my make-up done, even though my 6.15 slot might only last a minute. I think they paid me £150 a pop, but that's what you have to do to get on the ladder.

The funny thing is, Radio Suffolk really had to push me to do those commentaries, because I'd fallen out of love with football. If I couldn't play any more, I didn't want to watch any games. But having done two or three of them, I started enjoying it. I wasn't a big fan of travelling to and from the grounds, because Ipswich were playing all over the country and the traffic was often appalling, but once I had the mic in my hand and we went live, I was buzzing.

I also did a bit of work for Eurosport, which meant getting the Eurostar over to Paris for a job that paid me a few hundred quid. My first gig, I turned up to the studios and discovered I was working alongside Archie Macpherson, the legendary Scottish commentator. We were commentating on a friendly between Brazil and Mexico in Miami and the studio had a row of tiny boxes containing commentators from lots of different countries. Each box had a small TV screen, two sets of headphones and two mics, and it was very intimate indeed. Archie was pissed off from the outset because he thought the set-up was amateurish and no one had provided him with any team sheets. And the closer it got to kick-off, the more agitated he became: 'I don't know how they can do this to me. I have been doing this for decades and I am a professional.' He was right, but that didn't stop me finding it rather amusing.

We started going over a few of Brazil and Mexico's most recent games – who had scored, who had played well, that sort of stuff – but every thirty seconds or so Archie would shout to the guy at the fax machine, 'Have you got those team sheets yet?' And every time the guy would shout back, 'Not yet, Mr Macpherson!' In the end Archie was going ballistic, until eventually someone said, 'Sorry, Mr Macpherson, you're going live in thirty seconds.' So we rushed into the box, put our headphones on, grabbed our mics and the light went on.

Archie slipped into his commentary – 'Good evening from the Joe Robbie Stadium in Miami, and what a classic we have for you tonight, Brazil versus Mexico . . .' – before prompting me to say a few words. And the whole time I was talking, I was watching him watching the door, getting angrier and angrier and mouthing to the poor guy at the fax machine, 'Where's my teams?'

Having done a bit of scene-setting, and being in a mischievous mood, I said, 'I know a lot about this Brazilian side and what they can do – they've got the devastating strike partnership of Romario and Ronaldo, Cafu and Roberto Carlos at the back, the excellent Leonardo in midfield – but who do they have to fear from this Mexican team?' I couldn't resist, but Archie glared at me so hard I thought his eyes were going to pop out of his head. Suddenly, the door opened, Archie snatched the team sheets from the fax guy, and rattled off six or seven Mexican players. At the first break, he turned to me and said, 'If you ever do that again, son, you will never work in broadcasting again.'

I then landed a show on Anglia Television, co-hosting with a guy called Kevin Piper (a Norwich fan, but a lovely guy regardless), before BBC Radio 5 Live came in for me. Sky then poached me from the BBC to do co-commentaries on the Championship, or the First Division as it was then.

I hadn't thought about presenting until one day I received a call. The guy on the other end of the phone said he was from Talk Radio and asked if I could do a couple of hours for them on Wednesday night. I didn't really know what Talk Radio was, so I replied, 'A couple of hours of what?' And he said, 'Just chatting about the football.' That sounded like something I could do, so I promptly agreed.

By the Wednesday afternoon I'd forgotten all about it and was having a big lunch with a few friends in a curry house in Soho when my phone went again. This guy said to me, 'Alan, just phoning to remind you about tonight.'

'Tonight? What's happening tonight?'

'You agreed to do a couple of hours on Talk Radio.'

'Aah . . .'

'Where are you?'

'Don't worry, I'll be there.'

That was before Talk Radio had been rebranded as talkSPORT and when the studios were still on Oxford Street. So at about 6.40 I left the curry house and wandered over there with my old Spurs team-mate and big pal Paul 'Maxi' Miller. We turned up at 6.50, ten minutes before the show was due on air, and the first thing the producer Mike Parry, whom I'd never met before, said to me was, 'You're late. But thanks for coming.'

'Give us a break and just give me my script.'

'Script? There is no script. You go in the studio, sit at the mic, introduce yourself, and then the calls will start coming in.'

'You're having a laugh.'

'We haven't really got time for this . . .'

A few minutes later I was sat in this studio with Maxi, who wasn't even supposed to be there, sat next to me. And when it ticked over to seven o'clock and the red light went on, I just started talking: 'Good evening, Alan Brazil here. I hope you're all well. The traffic in London has been murder today, but I've managed to get myself to the studio and I'm happy to be joined by my good friend and former Spurs team-mate Paul Miller . . .'

I gave the number out at the first break and, to my

amazement, the phone lines lit up. For the next two hours Paul and I chatted about football to punters all over the country – cab drivers on their breaks, office workers on late shifts, bored blokes sat on their sofas watching the football on the telly – and it was just something that came naturally. I played football myself and enjoyed chatting about it. No sweat. The fact that I'd had two bottles of wine probably helped. People don't believe me when I tell them how it all started. But that's exactly how it happened: I wandered in with minutes to go, they put some cans on me, and off I went. Ever since that day I haven't looked back.

Before I knew it, I was hosting my own evening show. And when Talk Radio became talkSPORT in 2000, following its takeover by Kelvin MacKenzie's Wireless Group, they had a big clear-out of presenters and asked if I wanted to present the breakfast show. I knew the breakfast show on any radio station was the most important in terms of audience numbers, and I was very flattered to be asked, but I just didn't think it was for me. I struggled to get out of bed at 10 a.m. when I was playing football, so the thought of getting up at 3 a.m. every weekday filled me with dread. But they kept on at me, and eventually James Whale, a broadcasting legend who presented talkSPORT's night show, took me out for lunch in Canary Wharf and talked me into it. I'd been at Sky for five years, and I loved my time there with Andy Gray, Richard Keys and the boys, but it turned out to be the best move I ever made. It certainly worked out better than my move from Tottenham to United.

In those early days, talkSPORT was chaotic and many in the media world thought it would fail within a year. A big chunk of the old Talk Radio audience, who were used to and expected a diet of current affairs and news, disappeared overnight and even Kelvin MacKenzie started to think he'd wasted millions of pounds. But he ploughed on regardless. The BBC had most of the football tied up on the radio, apart from limited rights to the odd team in certain parts of the country, but Kelvin bought broadcasting rights for everything else, from cricket and boxing to golf and rugby. And soon listening figures started to rise again.

I'd presented with Mike 'Porky' Parry a couple of evenings a week on Talk Radio. He was now talkSPORT's programme director, but when he started coming on the breakfast show to review the newspapers, it reminded us that we had something special. So having chopped and changed my co-presenters for the first few months, they finally decided to make us a regular double act, fronting the show five days a week. Bear in mind, when I finished at ten o'clock, he still had his day job to do, running the rest of the station.

Porky had been news editor for the *Daily Express* and the Press Association, so he was a heavyweight journalist. He was a proper news hound, the kind of guy who would travel with a pair of pliers so that he could phone his story back to the newsroom before cutting the wire in the booth, thus preventing his rivals from using it. There are even stories about Porky spying on Mick Jagger in Mustique. But because he took himself very seriously, he was easy to wind up and the perfect punch-ball. I'd take the piss out of him for thinking he was an intellectual, despite attending a polytechnic. And when I started calling him 'Short Arms Porky', listeners believed me that he never bought a drink. Whenever we were at the Cheltenham Festival together, people would shout, 'Oi, Porky! Get the pints in, you tight git!'

Porky was a barmy character, a strange mix of the bonkers and the eminently sensible. He'd say the most ridiculous things. There was the time he remarked that horses should have wing mirrors, so that the jockeys could see behind them without having to turn around. He also said that they should make Tiger Woods play golf with a differently sized ball, and that he was worried that someone might shoot him, because he was too good and was going to win everything. At the time I thought he was saying all this stuff to get a rise. Now, I'm not so sure. And that really worries me. On another occasion he suggested that the royal family might have played a part in the death of Princess Diana, before adding, 'At least that's what Brazil always says.'

But Porky also knew a good story, sports or otherwise, and was always able to deliver a unique view on it. That was part of our successful formula, with me giving an ex-pro's view and him questioning and probing. And we weren't really insiders – we were comfortable being on the outside, having a pop and a dig at whoever and whatever we liked. Like all good journalists, Porky has got a hide as thick as a rhino and doesn't mind who he upsets.

Porky could blow hot and cold. He wanted things

done now and he wanted them done well, and we certainly had our ups and downs. But we worked well together, goading, bantering and bickering like an old married couple.

Kelvin might not have been able to secure football commentary rights, but Porky and I were soon being sent to England games all over Europe, including a friendly against Holland in Amsterdam in February 2002. Porky had already had loads of run-ins with the bosses, so before we left, Kelvin said to us, 'Behave yourselves. You cannot let us down.'

From the outset, Porky, who was technically my senior, behaved like my minder. We had a few drinks on the plane but when we arrived he suggested dinner in the hotel and a quiet night before the game the next day. Needless to say, that didn't happen. I was in Amsterdam and wanted to enjoy myself.

Having dropped off our bags at the hotel, we went straight over to an Italian restaurant and proceeded to drink nine bottles of Pinot Grigio (between four of us). I still intended to have an early night, but when we got back to the hotel and were having a nightcap in this cavernous lounge, in walked half of Fleet Street. It was *Sun* chief sportswriter John Sadler's last England game, and the rest of the reporters were giving him a big send-off. I knew quite a few of them because they'd covered my football career. Porky knew quite a few of them as well because he'd worked for various newspapers down the years. So bang went the early night.

The Fleet Street boys were only there for an hour or

so before heading off for a celebratory dinner, but now I had the taste. So despite Porky's protestations, I dragged him to a casino on Rembrandt Square, where some pals I'd met through my old Ipswich team-mate Frans Thijssen were having a card school. Once inside, I marched straight over to the roulette table and asked Porky for some money. He reached into his pocket, pulled out a wad of notes, and I grabbed the lot and gave them to the croupier, who furnished me with a tall stack of chips. Porky was now in a state of blind panic, which I was enjoying immensely. I said to him, 'Red or black?' When Porky blurted out 'Black!', I slid the chips across the table and the croupier spun the wheel. The ball did a few circuits before losing momentum, staggering here and there like a drunk man, and coming to a sudden halt. The number it had settled on was red. Porky was apoplectic. I thought he might hit me. I found it hilarious.

Porky having stormed off in a huff, I stayed on for a few beers and some cards. I don't know what time I left, but it wasn't early. Back at the hotel, I was halfway out of my jeans and just about to fall into bed when I heard a knock. I pulled my jeans back up, opened the door, and one of the production team, this Irish lad called Declan, was standing there looking worried. He said, 'Oh, sorry, Alan, you're already up. Mike told me to give you a shout.' Declan told Porky I was up and about and that I'd be down in a few minutes. But because it was only 4.30 and the show didn't start until six, I thought I could get an hour's sleep.

It felt like I'd only been asleep for a few seconds when there was a loud banging on my balcony window. It was

Declan again. It turned out that I'd fallen into a deep sleep and Porky had had to start the show without me. He'd done the first fifteen minutes and thrown to the travel, before telling Declan to get me out of bed. Declan sounded frantic – 'You've got to come, Alan! You've got to come! Porky's going mad!' – but I couldn't get out of bed, because my back had seized up.

Eventually I managed to separate myself from the mattress and get some clothes on, before almost crawling to the studio. But I was in no fit state to go on air. Luckily, there was a couch in the studio, so I lay down and watched Porky struggle through the show on his own. He was absolutely furious, as he had every right to be. But again, I couldn't help finding it funny. On the coffee table was a big bowl of Skittles, so I picked this bowl up, placed it on my belly and started popping them into my mouth. That didn't go down well with Porky. And he was even angrier when I started throwing them at his head: 'One for me . . . one for Porky . . . one for me . . . one for Porky . . .'

Having grabbed a few hours' sleep, had a shower and given myself a few slaps around the face, my back miraculously felt a lot easier. And after I'd ironed out my differences with Porky, whose bark was always worse than his bite and who never stayed angry for long, we decided to head over to the Italian restaurant again. When we walked through the door, the staff gave us a big round of applause. And our arrival just happened to coincide with a new delivery of stock, including a few cases of Gavi, which I am particularly partial to. So we had another long, meandering lunch, with various journalists, broadcasters and pundits popping in and out, and it was only when it got to seven o'clock that we remembered we had a football match to go to.

We paid up, said our goodbyes and jumped in a cab to the stadium. But when we arrived, all hell had already broken loose. There were fights breaking out all over the place, mounted police charging England fans, and Porky and I soon got split up. Suddenly alone on the streets of Amsterdam, I thought, 'What on earth am I doing here? It's cold and windy, I'm a Scotland supporter, and I don't even like watching England play.' So I flagged down a cab and headed back to the hotel. I watched the game in the lounge and got an early night. But the same couldn't be said for Porky, who went out drinking with a load of England fans after the 1-1 draw. On our return to England, Kelvin gave us such a bollocking and I almost got sacked – not for the last time.

I could write a whole book about the various scrapes Porky and I got ourselves into. The following year, 2003, Porky and I were sent to Seville for the UEFA Cup final between my beloved Celtic and José Mourinho's Porto. The trip didn't get off to the best of starts because the airport was about four hours' drive from Seville and we ended up hopelessly lost, at one point even crossing into Portugal. By the time we arrived at our hotel, I was ready for bed. I'd done the show that morning and had to be up again at five. But when we walked into the bar, it was full of mad Celtic fans, including some old school friends and mates from the city. There was absolutely no way I was going to bed now.

After a few drinks, Porky decided to retire to his room. But five minutes later he reappeared with a face like thunder, chuntering about finding a couple of Scotsmen in his bed. I had to explain that I'd given his room to an old pal of mine who was over with his elderly father-in-law. The fact that I had two beds in my room quelled Porky's anger, but only slightly.

The following afternoon we were having a few bevvies when Porky said to me, 'Drink up, Al, or we'll miss the start of the game.'

I took a deep breath and replied, 'Mike, there's something I need to tell you.'

Porky looked worried.

'You know those two guys who were in your room last night?'

'How could I forget.'

'Well, I also gave them our tickets.'

Porky thought I was joking. I wasn't. Then I said, 'And we haven't got a room tonight, either.' We ended up watching the game in the bar and stayed up all night, despite Celtic losing 3-2. I don't think Porky spoke to me once.

I have a habit of missing major events. In December 2007 me and my breakfast co-presenter Ronnie Irani were sent to the Ricky Hatton–Floyd Mayweather fight in Las Vegas and had ringside seats. But when I walked into the MGM Grand Garden Arena I got so much abuse from Hatton's followers, many of whom were Manchester City fans, I walked straight out again. We were also sent to the Hatton–Manny Pacquiao fight in

May 2009 at the same venue. On the afternoon of the fight we went to the Bellagio for drinks and a bit of a gamble. I won a bit, lost a bit, won it back again, before bumping into a guy I went to school with and hadn't seen for decades. I had a couple of drinks with my old mate, then went back to my room for a shower, before heading back downstairs for a bite to eat. More people joined us, we had a few more drinks, and suddenly someone tapped me on the shoulder and said, 'How was the fight?' He'd spotted the pass around my neck.

I replied, 'What do you mean? I'm going after this drink.'

'Alan,' he said, 'it's already happened. Hatton got knocked out in the second round.'

We were meant to come home the following day, but I'd met so many people I knew from London I decided to stay a bit longer. When I finally got back I got yet another rap across the knuckles, as well as another five grand fine.

Once, I missed almost an entire Test match. The decision to send us to Brisbane for the first Test of the 2017/18 Ashes was very much last-minute, so the flight cost £11,000. Not only did I have my own bed, I also had my own shower. Not that I used either of them. I spent most of the flight from Singapore to Brisbane drinking a beautiful Napa Valley red. The flight attendant kept saying to me, 'Would you like me to make your bed, sir?' And I kept replying, 'No thank you, I'm watching some films. The only thing you have to look out for is if my glass is empty.' When they announced that we were starting our descent, the attendant said, 'Can I get you anything? We might be circling for twenty minutes because it's very busy.' When I asked for another glass of red, she replied, 'I'm sorry, sir, we've run out. You've drunk all four bottles.'

We broadcast the show from a pub round the corner from the ground, surrounded by Barmy Army England fans. But I only watched the first hour of the first day of the Test. The rest of the time I spent in my hotel room, suffering with a terrible dose of jetlag.

It should be noted that when Porky and I landed ourselves in trouble, it wasn't always my fault. In early May 2018, former Liverpool and Wales striker Dean Saunders, fellow presenter Ian 'The Moose' Abrahams and I went to Rome for the second leg of Liverpool's Champions League semi-final against Roma. On the morning of the game we presented the show from a rooftop bar overlooking the Spanish Steps, before getting stuck into some champagne on the terrace below. It was all nice and relaxed, until some Liverpool fans decided to drop a water bomb on us. The poor woman on the table next to us almost jumped out of her skin.

It was a good job we didn't react, because these Liverpool fans were also filming it. But what annoyed me more than the actual incident was when I found out that one of the producers had taken the footage and published it on talkSPORT's Twitter feed. I refused to do the show the following morning. When I was finally persuaded to go on, about forty minutes in, Dean asked me if I'd watched the game. When I told him I hadn't, and that I'd listened to it on the radio instead, Dean replied, 'What, in Italian?'

Then there was the time Porky almost got filled in by an elderly Scottish gentleman at York races. We were in York for the Ebor Festival and had an unbelievable two days. The organizers are always so welcoming. Whether it's William Derby, the chief executive and clerk of the course, or any of the other people running the festival, they always go out of their way to make our stay as comfortable as possible and love coming on the show to chat about racing.

We did the show from the course on Thursday and Friday, then went for a walk across the Knavesmire, which is where the racecourse is situated and York gallows used to be. I am reliably informed that Dick Turpin was hanged there. After our walk we headed back to our hotel, had a club sandwich and a couple more drinks, and Porky ended up pissed. And when I say pissed, I mean absolutely legless, which is never a good thing. This is a man who will read every page of every newspaper in the country, every day of the week, and has an encyclopaedic knowledge about almost everything. But as soon as he gets a couple of bottles of Pinot Grigio inside him, he turns into an absolute nightmare who thinks he's heavyweight champion of the world.

Just as we were heading off to bed, this oldish gentleman walked in with a stunning woman on his arm who could have been his daughter. This guy might have been knocking on a bit, but he was one of those handsome older guys with swept-back greying hair and a deep suntan. He was also dressed immaculately and had a great big watch on his wrist. Anyway, as soon as Porky clocked them, he staggered over and slurred, 'Oi! Excuse me, my friend. How's your daughter? Is it your daughter?'

The guy smiled at him, but I was so embarrassed. I apologized for Porky's behaviour, grabbed him by the shoulders and hissed 'What is wrong with you?' before trying to bundle him into the lift. Unfortunately, Porky wasn't having it. Instead, he sat in the corner of the bar giggling, pointing at this couple and saying, 'Look at those two. Ridiculous . . .'

After a few minutes, this beautiful woman got up and went to the loo. And as she walked past, Porky said, 'You're wasting your time tonight, darling. I'd get the old boy off to bed and then come back down and have a good time with me.' This woman was quite rightly pissed off, and I wasn't particularly happy either. In fact, I could have killed him. Again I apologized profusely and tried to persuade Porky to go to bed, but he still wasn't listening to me.

A couple of minutes later, the guy got up to go to the loo. Porky went to say something else to him but the guy leant over, grabbed him by the throat and growled in a Scottish accent, 'I might be seventy-two, but you're having it.' With that, he pulled his head back, as if he was about to stick the nut on him. I managed to get between them, apologized again – 'I'm so sorry about him. He doesn't mean it. He's had two days in the sun and too much to drink' – and the guy backed off. I used the fact that we were both from Scotland to break the ice, before manoeuvring him to the other end of the bar, as far away from Porky as possible. For the first few minutes he kept looking at Porky, as if he wanted to go back and have another go. But once I'd convinced him he wasn't worth it – which he wasn't – we had a nice chat and a couple of drinks. I'm sure Porky would have enjoyed his company, had he not been preposterously drunk and insulted him and his wife.

Along with my media work, I've also done a lot of after-dinner speaking. Like most people, I was very nervous when I started doing it. It can be very intimidating, standing up there with a microphone in your hand in front of hundreds of people wanting to be entertained after a skinful of beer. As with everything else in my post-football career, no one taught me how to do it, I just had to work it out for myself. Now, I don't have a problem – it just comes naturally. And if I ever stop doing radio, I could probably make a living from after-dinner speaking alone. I can turn up pretty much anywhere – lunches, dinners, charity auctions – and just tell stories.

There are sometimes one or two grumpy people who would have preferred to listen to someone else, or to chat among themselves, but most of the time the company is great. If it's a corporate do, it will more often than not be in the City. They usually go down a storm, because people who work in the City tend to be into their sport. I have a nice dinner and a bit of wine, stand up at the end, tell a few football and horseracing stories, drop a few famous names, and that's me done. Easy-peasy.

More recently I've been doing a few private lunches, with twenty or thirty people. Because they're more intimate, I can get to know the people better and have a bit of banter while telling my tales.

I've done a fair bit of after-dinner speaking on my own, but I prefer to do shows with other people. Nowadays I do a lot of gigs with Ray Parlour and Ally McCoist. They've both got lots of stories as well, so we'll reel a few off, take questions from the audience and interact. People love it. The venues get sold out and we get standing ovations. But back in the day, Porky was my sidekick. And the problem with Porky was that he used to get very nervous.

We once did a gig at a golf club local to me in Suffolk. In the pub beforehand, Porky suddenly stopped speaking and went very pale. When I asked him if he was OK, he just stared straight through me. When we got to the dinner at the golf club I went on and did my bit, which went down great, before Porky came on after me. But when he stood up, all he was able to say was, 'Hi. I'm Mike Parry from talkSPORT.' Then there was silence. After about ten excruciating seconds, I had to go up and have a quick chat to him, after which he just walked off like a zombie. Things got even worse for Porky when the comedian they'd hired got up and slaughtered him, which I obviously found hilarious.

Another time, Crystal Palace put on an end-of-season dinner to thank their supporters. They put a massive tent on the pitch at Selhurst Park and the plan was for me and Porky to stand up and tell a few tales after everyone had eaten. Simon Jordan was the owner of Palace at the time but, for whatever reason, he wasn't present. I'd agreed with Porky that I'd do four stories and he'd do two, but as soon as he got the mic in his hands that plan went straight out of the window. He forgot about the stories he was supposed to be doing and started talking a stream of bollocks, before singing this incomprehensible ditty about Simon Jordan. As I said, Porky liked to have a few drinks to calm the nerves.

And just when I thought things couldn't get any more surreal, Porky said, 'Hands up who hates the chairman?'

I couldn't believe what I was hearing, although most people found it funny and a few hands did go up.

It was then that I noticed this massive guy wearing a long leather coat and leather gloves – he looked like Lennox Lewis's big brother – hovering at the side of the stage and signalling for Porky to sit down. When Porky didn't sit down, this bloke climbed on the stage and started saying, 'Off, off, off.' Porky blundered on, and eventually one of the Palace bigwigs stood up and told him to wind it up.

When I got up there again, I apologized for Porky's behaviour, explained that he'd got a bit excited and wished them good luck for the following season. I thought I'd smoothed things over, but while we were laughing along to the comedian we were suddenly surrounded by four or five security guards. One of them growled, 'You are wanted in the boardroom.'

When we walked into the boardroom, this scruffy-looking bloke was sitting at the end of this long table, looking very pissed off. Before we'd even had a chance to say hello, he said, 'How dare you accept our invitation and our hospitality and then insult my brother.' It was only then that I realized this bloke must be Dominic Jordan.

Suddenly, Porky said, 'It's all right, let's all have a drink.'

Dominic didn't look like he was in the mood to be cracking open any champagne, so I went behind the bar and poured two beers for me and Porky. Bear in mind I'd done nothing wrong; this predicament was all of Porky's making. A bit of an argument ensued, before Dominic called us a disgrace and stormed out of the room. And we weren't able to savour our beer: Lennox Lewis's big brother was standing by the door, staring straight at us.

Having managed to get out of the room without being garrotted, we were followed down the stairs by four goons. When we got outside, I whispered to Porky 'Do not say a word' before turning round to the goons and saying, 'Is one of you David?'

'Yeah.'

'Dominic said you'd drop us at Croydon station.'

'Really?'

'Yeah. Did you not hear him? Do you want me to get him back?'

'No. I'll get the keys.'

When the guy reappeared behind the wheel of this tiny car, we jumped in and he whisked us off to the station.

When he'd driven off, Porky said to me, 'When did Dominic say anything about giving us a lift?'

'He didn't,' I told him. 'I made it up. Otherwise, they might have filled us in.'

Porky and I jumped on the train and I berated him all the way back to central London: 'Parry, you're a numptie. I told you the plan and once again you went off on a rant. You're lucky we got out of there alive.'

I tried to apologize to Simon Jordan on behalf of Porky, but he wasn't interested in talking about it. However, when Simon became a talkSPORT presenter, we became good pals. He's got a place in Marbella, so we meet up for a drink when I'm over there. He's been great for talkSPORT. He's honest and frank and gives a different perspective. We're always hearing from players and managers but having a former owner talk about the business side of football – transfer negotiations, player contracts, agents – is fascinating for listeners.

Of course, after attending the 2004 Cheltenham Festival, I did finally get the sack. By that stage Kelvin MacKenzie had started to lose trust in Porky and me. He thought we were enjoying ourselves a bit too much (we were certainly enjoying ourselves, but I never saw it as a problem, as long as we were performing on air and pulling in the listeners). So before the festival, Porky said to me, 'We cannot blow this. Otherwise this might be the last outside broadcast we ever do.' As was the way with Porky, sometimes he got things almost right.

I absolutely love the Cheltenham Festival. It's the World Cup of racing and one of the highlights of my year, right up there with Christmas with the family. The course is stunning, the company – which largely consists of tens of thousands of visiting Irish people, with bulging wallets and a tremendous love of life – is about as good as it gets, and the people in charge are always very welcoming. We do the show from London on the Monday, drive straight down to Cheltenham, check into the hotel, have a curry, and then get to the track at 5.40 a.m. on the Tuesday to do the show from there. It will still be quite murky and eerie at that time in the morning, but soon the sun will come up over Cleeve Hill and the place will come alive. It gives me goose pimples just thinking about it.

Back in the day, we'd broadcast from Lord Vestey's private box. The 3rd Baron Vestey, a big cheese in butchery, was chairman of the course and the perfect host. Every time we turned up, his box would be fully stocked with the finest wines and champagnes. Out of politeness I'd also bring some bubbly along, and mid-show, at 8 a.m., the tradition was to throw to the news and pop a bottle. I'd pop a bottle on Tuesday, Porky would pop a bottle on Wednesday, it would be me again on Thursday, and Porky again on Friday.

But one day, Porky forgot to bring any champagne. I said to him, 'What do you mean? How could you forget the champagne? That's the most important part of the day.' So after doing some scene-setting – 'Cheltenham is silent, but the sun is coming up over Cleeve Hill and soon the horses will leave the stables, the punters will start pouring in and the place will come alive' – I said to Porky, 'Get your fat arse under the table and find some bubbly. There has to be some under there.'

Porky did as he was told, and just as I was waiting to come back after the news and sport headlines, the door opened and in walked this guy looking immaculate in his morning suit and top hat. Right on cue, Porky reappeared, triumphantly clutching two bottles of champagne. And when he saw our new arrival, he started blabbering away in the most degrading manner: 'Oh, my lordship. I'm so, so sorry. I left two bottles in the taxi and was going to replace these two with even better champagne. Not that that's possible, obviously, given that your champagne is the best in the whole of Cheltenham . . .' He must have been down on his knees for about three minutes, while I was pissing myself laughing. Eventually, this guy in the morning suit and top hat said, 'Parry, get up, you prat. I'm Lord Vestey's chauffeur.'

Once a show was done, we'd have a two-minute breather before wandering over to the Guinness Village, which is more of a small city. It was also the tradition, and still is, that I'd drink the first pint of Guinness of the week, at about 10.17. Two gulps and it's gone. And before I know it I've got ten pints lined up on the bar, bought by I don't know who.

The box holders are allowed in at 10.30, everyone else at eleven, and soon the place is thronging. Nowadays, the usual gang – me, Ally McCoist, a couple of lads from Coral bookmakers and maybe a producer and sound engineer – congregate in the corner by Arthur's Bar (it's almost become a ritual) and soon we'll be joined by various ex-footballers, business people, City types and old mates from Holyrood School in Glasgow. On top of that there will be people I haven't met for years, people who know such-and-such person who knows so-and-so's relative or old friend, and hundreds of talkSPORT fans, who will have been listening to the show on their way to the course. The Irish band will be fiddling away, everyone will be singing, selfies will be taken left, right and centre, the banter will be flying and the laughs will be loud.

When the company is that great and the atmosphere so heady, drinking Guinness is like drinking water. By the time I get out of the tent at about 12.30 I'll already have had a dozen pints, on top of the champagne. I'll spend the rest of the day meeting people for lunch and doing the rounds of executive boxes, because I can never turn down an invitation. And in every one of those boxes individual parties will be going on. I'll sink more champagne, place a few bets, gather round the TV to watch the latest race, soak up the roar of the crowd, and hopefully back a few winners.

Sometimes in the early years I went to bed too late. My head would hit my pillow at 1.30 a.m., I'd have a few hours' sleep and be back on the course at 5.40. By the Thursday I'd be talking Greek on air. Which brings us back to 2004, the year it all went wrong.

Kelvin and the talkSPORT bean counters decided that we had to broadcast the show from London the day after the festival ended, which meant having to pack up the studio in Lord Vestey's box as soon as we were done on the Thursday, leaving Cheltenham early, in order to get ahead of the traffic, and missing the Gold Cup. As you can imagine, I thought this decision was madness, and told them so.

The Gold Cup is the festival's main event, what the festival is all about, so there was no way I was missing it. So after the show on Thursday I thanked Lord Vestey for his hospitality, put a few bets on and headed to the Guinness tent. When Porky, who now had his sensible head on, tried to persuade me to leave with him, I told him I wasn't coming. And once Porky had gone, I easily slipped back into the groove. Before I walked into that tent I was flagging. But now I was flying again. Former footballers and Sky pundits Chris Kamara and Alan McInally were in there, as well as Jim Lewis, the owner of Best Mate, who would win his third successive Gold Cup later that day. I was backing winners, including Best Mate, and loving every second. London could wait.

However, after the last race at 5.45, reality suddenly dawned on me. I had a car, but there was no way I was going to be able to drive home. So I was going to have to find somewhere to stay the night, find someone to take me there, get up at some ungodly hour and drive back to London.

Because all the hotels in Cheltenham were rammed, I had to stay in a lovely little Cotswolds village called Moreton-in-Marsh, about 25 miles away. I'd just bought a new phone which wasn't working – the on-off button had jammed – which meant I didn't have an alarm. So when I checked into this little hotel, I said to the wee Irish lad on reception, 'I need you to wake me up at 3.30 a.m. If you wake me up then, I should be able to make it back to London in time for the show.' This lad assured me that wouldn't be a problem and I retired with a glass of red wine to this cosy little room with a big roaring fire.

But just as I was about to go to bed, this lad walked in and said, 'I'm surprised you're not down the road.'

'Why's that?'

'A former Scottish footballer owns the pub. You probably know him.'

The guy in question was Jim Steele, who won the FA Cup with Southampton in 1976 and played with two of my good mates from the world of football and horses, former England striker and trainer Mick Channon and Alan Ball, who won the World Cup with England and was now a huge racing fan. How could I resist? What could possibly go wrong? I said to the wee Irish lad, 'Right, I'll go and have a couple. But don't forget the 3.30 alarm call.'

When I walked into the pub, Jim was standing behind the bar wearing a Rangers shirt. I couldn't believe my eyes. I knew he was a Rangers fan, but this was the day after St Patrick's Day and the place was full of Celtic fans, singing Irish songs. Jim didn't see me, so I sat at the end of the bar and joined in with the singing. But after a couple of pints, I shouted across the bar, 'Oi, Bluenose! I need eight more pints of Guinness over here!'

I knew Jim could hear me and was doing his best to ignore me, but after some more provocation he snapped and roared, 'Right, who's the big mouth?' Jim could always handle himself and was quite intimidating when he wanted to be. But when he saw me, he broke into a big smile and said, 'Alan Brazil! I don't believe it!' We hugged across the bar, before a large glass of wine was thrust into my hand. There was more singing of Irish songs, more swapping of football stories and many more tales of bets won and lost.

Next thing I knew I was awake in my bed, staring at the ceiling. And I had this horrible feeling in the pit of my stomach that something was wrong. I turned on the bedside lamp, looked at my watch and couldn't believe my eyes: it was 4.40, I was still in the Cotswolds, and the show was starting in London at six. I rolled off the bed, grabbed my bag, threw my clothes on and rushed down to reception, where the same wee Irish lad was sat behind the desk. There was a grandfather clock standing against the wall, so I pointed at it and screamed, 'Look at the time! It's 4.45! I told you to wake me at 3.30! I'm never going to make it to London for the start of the show!'

This lad kept trying to say something and I kept cutting him off, but just as I was walking out of the door, he shouted, 'But you didn't get home until 3.50!'

There was no time for an inquest. I apologized for having a go at him and flounced out of the hotel, only to find that my car was blocked in by a milk float and the milkman was refusing to move it. By the time we'd finished arguing, it was almost five. I couldn't call the office because my mobile was knackered, but I still thought I might be able to make it, even though it would have been impossible in a Ferrari on deserted roads. I did think about calling the office from a payphone, but the number was stored in my mobile, which I couldn't even switch on.

The first thing I did when I got back to London that evening was head to the shop that sold me this dodgy phone, threw it across the counter and blamed the poor bloke for getting me the sack. That was my mindset at the time, blaming everyone but myself for the predicament I'd landed myself in. With the new mobile they gave me I phoned my daughter to tell her what had gone on and the first thing she said was, 'Dad, Mum is going to kill you. You're in a lot of trouble.'

It was my wife's birthday, so I was obviously in the doghouse and felt bad about ruining her day. But I very rarely get down for long, so I replied, 'Don't worry about that. Get the skis out – we're going to Meribel.' I ended the call, headed to my favourite wine bar on Ludgate Hill and ordered champagne. A day later, I was on the slopes of Meribel, loving life again.

But a few days after that I switched on my mobile for the first time since leaving England and saw that I had about a hundred missed calls from Porky. And seconds later, he called again. Porky and I had been through so much together over the previous few years, but now he didn't sound too friendly. To be fair, I wasn't too friendly either, because I was still in blame mode. I was calling him a snake and telling him that none of it would have happened if he hadn't deserted me (which was bollocks, of course). Then he suddenly said, 'Al, I'm afraid we've got to sack you. I'm cancelling your contract.'

There was no point arguing about it. As talkSPORT's programme director, Porky was officially my boss. And he was acting under orders from MacKenzie, so I wasn't going to change his mind. So I simply replied, 'Well, there's not a lot I can do about that, except to say that it was great working with you.'

Initially, I was shell-shocked. I'd had one of the best jobs in broadcasting, a job I absolutely loved, and now I was unemployed – and on a very expensive skiing trip. My wife was extremely worried, but I didn't dwell on it for long. I'd had a few big setbacks in my life, not least when my football career was cut short by injury when I was only twenty-seven. So I did what I often do in a crisis: popped a bottle of champagne and told myself that something would come up.

When I returned home from Meribel there was a brown envelope waiting for me on the doorstep. It was the official notice of my sacking. I understood why Kelvin had to send a letter, but this letter was just nasty and completely uncalled for. He even called me 'a disgrace to my family'.

I should point out that Kelvin was a brilliant journalist and very generous. If we were bringing in big listening figures, he'd give us all a big bonus. And he once phoned me on New Year's Eve to thank me for saving his radio station. But he had a reputation as a hard-nosed operator who didn't mess about. Porky, who worked under Kelvin at the *Sun* and absolutely revered him, used to get bollocked by Kelvin all the time. Sometimes that was horrible to watch, sometimes it was hilarious. But what made me lose some respect for Kelvin was the fact that he never had the bottle to say difficult things to my face, probably because he knew I'd tell him to piss off. Instead, he'd always send a letter, or use Porky instead.

Having retreated to my home in Suffolk, offers started to come in. There were a few calls from newspapers and betting websites, which were starting to get big. Radio 5 Live also made contact and we spoke a bit about doing a show for them. But one day I was sitting in a hotel called Milsoms when my phone rang. When I flipped the phone open, Porky's name was on the screen. I didn't want to speak to him. Not that I blamed Porky for what had happened, I just wasn't really interested in discussing it. But after a few rings, I answered.

After a bit of awkward small talk, Porky said, 'Listen, it's bad. We're getting thousands of emails. People are genuinely upset that we sacked you. We need you to come back.'

I'd been replaced on the breakfast show by a guy called Paul Breen-Turner, a regular talkSPORT contributor who was based in Spain. Paul was a pal of mine whose Spanish studio we'd broadcast from and with whom I'd shared plenty of beers. He was also a good broadcaster, but obviously wasn't catching the public's imagination. I have to admit I was astonished by the reaction to my sacking, but wasn't sure whether Kelvin would have me back. Porky, however, was certain he could persuade him to change his mind.

A couple of days later I met up with Porky and agreed to return in principle, after which there were lots of phone calls and meetings with various talkSPORT bigwigs. Meanwhile, whenever I went out people were asking me when I was going back, to which I'd usually reply, 'We'll have to see.' Then, about ten days after returning from Meribel, Kelvin gave me my job back. As part of his compromise deal I'd get fined £5,000 for failing to complete a programme. That sounded fair to me.

At the time of writing I've outlasted Kelvin by fifteen years. In 2005, a little over a year after he sacked me, Kelvin's Wireless Group was bought out by Northern Irish media company UTV and he left the building. Funny how things work out.

At the 2010 Cheltenham Festival I landed myself in trouble with management again. I don't know which bright spark decided it was a good idea to have me present the show from a bar, but that's what happened. To add insult to injury, the bosses had decided to replace me at the course with Richard Keys and Andy Gray. I told all my mates to come and visit me at the pub, and one morning a friend from the Isle of Dogs walked in with his girlfriend and plonked a bottle of champagne down in front of me.

I popped this bottle at about eight o'clock, as was the tradition at Cheltenham, and the following day I got an email from the programme director, asking if I'd been drinking during the show. When I told him that of course I'd been drinking during the show, and that I do it every year, he was flabbergasted and launched an inquiry. I said to them, 'You put me in a pub and I had a couple of drinks. So what? You can't sack me for that.' I even made them listen to the tapes, to prove that I wasn't the slightest bit drunk. And after one day off the air, which I might call a mini-sacking, I was reinstated.

There's obviously something about Cheltenham that makes me lose focus. Some cynics might say it's black and white and served in a glass. After Laura Woods's first show with me at Cheltenham, I persuaded her to join me for a couple of pints in the Guinness tent. Despite feeling a little bit delicate the following morning, she agreed to join my wife and me for lunch that afternoon. It got to about three o'clock and Laura was nowhere to be seen. And when I fished my phone out of my pocket, I had loads of texts and missed calls from her. I forgot that I'd booked two tables in two VIP tents, just in case.

When Laura finally arrived at the owners' and trainers' restaurant in the paddock, me and Ally were talking to Sir Alex Ferguson, who was there with the Rolling Stones' Ronnie Wood and the businessman Ged Mason, with whom Fergie owned horses. We had a great day at the course, before heading to a party in a big manor house nearby. Somehow, Laura managed to get Fergie to sing karaoke, which is not something I ever thought

I'd see. If I remember rightly, his chosen song was John Denver's 'Leaving On A Jet Plane'.

I've been lucky enough to present my talkSPORT show not just from Cheltenham but from racecourses all over the country and beyond, and they're some of my most cherished memories as a broadcaster. Wherever I go, they treat me like a king. At Ayr, where the Scottish Grand National is run, they give me a suite at the hotel on the racecourse and my room always has a bottle of champagne, an ice bucket, a big bunch of flowers and even a framed photo of me with the UEFA Cup. That's how to welcome someone!

Royal Ascot is also a great gig. We broadcast from a box overlooking the winning line, and because I'm on air so early, I watch the place come alive. But it's also a tough gig, because we arrive on the Monday and the meeting runs from Tuesday to Saturday. It's not so much the broadcasting that kills me, it's all the socializing that takes place afterwards. By Thursday, my voice is usually cracking up, because I've spent the previous four days talking non-stop.

A few years ago I attended the Prix de l'Arc de Triomphe in Paris for talkSPORT. I went over with a guy called Ozzie and TV tipster Mark Winstanley, aka 'Couch', who is a big Chelsea supporter, very quick-witted and very funny company. They told me that we were getting the Eurostar at 11.30 a.m., so as soon as I finished the show on Friday morning I threw off my headphones, jumped in the lift, practically ran out of the building and hailed a cab. When I arrived at St Pancras, sweating and in a bit of a panic because we'd hit a bit of traffic, Ozzie and Couch suggested we retire to the champagne bar.

'Champagne bar? I thought we had to get on the train?'

'Not until three o'clock. But we know what you're like when you have a few drinks straight after the show. We were worried you'd never make it.'

I wasn't very happy that they'd got me there on false pretences. In fact, I was quite pissed off. But I made the most of it. And by the time we got on the train, we were smashed. I don't know how many bottles of champagne we drank, but it was more than one. Paris isn't far from London but I bumped into a lot of people I knew, including the trainer George Baker, and spent the whole time in the bar. I had a first-class ticket but didn't sit down once.

After arriving at Gare du Nord, we got in the taxi queue and it didn't move for half an hour. So Ozzie and Couch suggested we get the Metro instead. I said, 'I'm not getting the Metro, I'll get lost. There must be a problem. Maybe there's been an accident or terrorist incident. I'm going to sit in that brasserie over there, have a few more glasses of wine and wait for the queue to go down.' So Ozzie and Couch jumped on the Metro and left me to it.

When I returned to the taxi queue, it was even worse. After making enquiries, I discovered that it was the end of Paris Fashion Week, as well as the start of the Arc meeting. So I joined the back of the queue and resigned myself to a long wait.

After a few minutes, some guy wandered over and said, 'Monsieur, monsieur, motorcycle taxi?'

'What? No thank you. I'm not getting on the back of a motorbike.'

About every twenty minutes a taxi would turn up, one person would get in – two at most – and everyone would shuffle forward a few inches. I kept staring at the Metro sign and thinking 'Should I risk it?' before eventually heading back to the brasserie for more wine. But when I returned to the queue for a second time it had got even longer. The same bloke came over with a big smile on his face, asked me again if I wanted a ride on the back of his motorcycle taxi, and I told him to piss off, in the politest possible way.

However, half an hour later I was still in the queue and it was still barely moving. So I finally cracked and said to the motorcycle taxi man, who had never stopped smiling at me imploringly, 'How much to the InterContinental Champs-Élysées?'

'Sixty euro.'

'You're on.'

If only it had been that simple. He had one of those massive BMW bikes, like the ones the police and paramedics use, and I'd had quite a lot to drink, so I couldn't get on it. He called over a mate, and after something of a struggle, as if I was trying to mount a racehorse, they finally got me in the saddle. But now they couldn't find a helmet big enough for my head. They both went hunting for an extra large, and after about ten minutes they returned with one they thought might do the job. But even this helmet wasn't quite big enough, so they had to balance it on top of my head and hammer it on with their fists. They got it on eventually, but nearly took my ears off in the process.

Despite the initial ignominy, the actual ride was wonderful. We skated right through the Paris traffic like a hot knife through butter, and were at the hotel in twenty minutes. My wife Jill was in Paris with another couple and I thought they'd be in the bar and pissed off waiting for me. But they were nowhere to be seen. And when I went to check in, the receptionist said to me, 'Sorry, sir, but you don't appear to have a reservation.'

'Is this the InterContinental Champs-Élysées?'

'Yes.'

'Well, this must be the right hotel; my wife's already checked in.'

'Oh. Hold on. There are two InterContinentals. We have a sister hotel further down the road, it must be that one.'

'Great. How do I get there? I'm not getting a taxi.'

'Don't worry, we have our own driver. Go back to the bar and I'll let you know when he's here.'

I spent another half an hour drinking in the bar before the car turned up and whisked me to this other hotel. My wife and the other couple weren't downstairs, so I checked in and went up to my room. When I walked in, I could hear Jill having a shower. And because it was now quite late, I jumped straight into bed. But just as I was dozing off, the bathroom door opened and this strange bloke came wandering out with a towel around his waist.

At which point, all hell broke loose.

He was screaming at me to get out and I was screaming at him, while trying to see if Jill was in the bathroom. In no time it got a little bit aggressive, we started wrestling, and I eventually got this bloke in an armlock. I was bollock naked and he was bollock naked, because his towel had fallen off.

While we were still in this semi-passionate embrace, I heard a knocking at the door and someone saying, 'Monsieur? Monsieur? Is there anything wrong?' Me and this bloke immediately ceased hostilities, and when I opened the door I found the manager and my missus standing in the corridor. The numpties had given me the wrong key. Poor bloke, finding a naked me on his bed. But spare a thought for me too: I thought Jill was having an affair with him!

As you can imagine, it took me quite a while to calm down after that. Once I had, I realized I'd left most of my money on the sideboard in the bloke's room. I was too embarrassed to go back, so at least he earned a few quid from the fight. That was my first day in Paris for the Arc, and a day that could only happen to me. But what a great weekend it would turn out to be.

Some of the talkSPORT trips have been cracking simply because they should, by rights, have gone so badly wrong. In 2018 they sent a few of us over to Paris to cover the Ryder Cup. It was me, Ally McCoist and Niall Horan from One Direction, who is a big golf fan and had been on the show quite a few times. It was all booked quite late, so we ended up in this little hotel in Montrouge, which is a suburb in the south of the city. And because they hadn't sorted any accreditation for Ally, we had no choice but to cover the golf from the hotel.

On day one we set ourselves up in the lobby and started broadcasting from there. But after an hour or so the manager marched over and told us he was going to pull the plug, because we were making too much noise and other guests were complaining. I begged him not to kick us out and told him we were plugging his hotel to millions of people back in the UK, which gave us a reprieve until the end of that show. But on day two we had to move the studio to this little AstroTurf garden outside my bedroom window.

Me, McCoist and Horan emptied the minibar and broadcast the last two days of the Ryder Cup from that roof, without seeing a ball being hit. There was a TV showing the golf in my room, but we didn't bother watching it. We'd talk about everything else that was going on and occasionally throw to Rupert Bell on the course, who'd give us an update.

Talking of hushed commentary, I once covered the Open Championship from Royal Lytham. After I'd finished my show, the producer said to me, 'Alan, we've lost contact with two of our on-course reporters. Could you do us a favour and follow Colin Montgomerie for a hole or two?' I was fine with that, until they strapped this big backpack on me and handed me a brick-like walkie-talkie with a 10ft aerial. I looked like a Navy Seal.

Anyway, there I was, creeping around and whispering like golf commentators do – 'Here's Monty with an eagle putt at thirteen' – when the sun suddenly came out. So now I was wearing three layers, including waterproofs, and it was about 80 degrees. I was sweating buckets and panting like a dog, the backpack was stuck to me, and I thought to myself, 'I've had enough. I'm not doing this any more.' Just then I spotted a gap in the boundary fence running next to the railway line and thought, 'Hang on a minute, my digs are behind that fence.' So I let Monty and his playing partners tee off, stripped down and squeezed through this gap, which was a miracle in itself.

I made my way back to my digs and was about to climb in the shower when I could just about hear someone saying, 'Let's go to the fourteenth, where Colin Montgomerie is putting for birdie. Alan Brazil, how long has Monty got?' So I grabbed the mic and started making interference noises, punctuated with the occasional 'Can you hear me?' I could hear the producer saying, 'I told you the transmitter on that side of the course isn't good enough! Get hold of an engineer and get him out to Alan! Alan? Alan? You're very faint . . .'

I thought, 'Bollocks to this, I'm not going back out there,' and that was me for the day. The poor engineer got such a bollocking and it wasn't even his fault. I never owned up to the producer, because she would have got violent. But I did tell the powers that be, and they pissed themselves laughing.

At the 2014 Ryder Cup at Gleneagles we somehow ended up sharing a house with Brian McFadden from Westlife and the *Dragons' Den* businessman Peter Jones. One night I bumped into Brian in a local hotel and we were soon doing a karaoke version of 'Flower Of Scotland', with everyone joining in. It was only later I discovered that we'd inadvertently gatecrashed a wedding.

Back at the house, me and Brian were singing in the kitchen when a couple of strangers wandered in. When I asked what they were doing, they told me they were there to produce *Weekend Sports Breakfast*. When I asked what time it was, they replied in unison, 'Quarter past five.' I just about had time for thirty minutes' sleep.

7

My First Love

As you may have guessed by now, I love absolutely everything about racing – the horses, the jockeys, the owners, the trainers, all the other personalities connected to it, the gambling, the winning, the losing, the wining and dining. I don't care if I'm being entertained by a Greek shipping magnate, plied with champagne by a lord or eating sandwiches from the boot of a car – it's all the same to me.

I live near Thurlow Estate, where they have point-to-pointing – racing over fences for hunting horses and amateur riders – and I never miss a meeting. The whole family, including the grandchildren, heads over there with a picnic hamper and we have a brilliant day. If I had to choose between racing and football for the rest of my life, racing would romp home.

The first time I went to the races was when my mum's brother-in-law took me to Lanark when I was a kid (Lanark Racecourse closed in 1977, so it shows you how long ago that was). I remember thinking, 'This is different, this is fun.' Occasionally I'd bunk off school and watch the racing on TV, but it wasn't until I moved to Ipswich that I started to understand it and got hooked.

And at some point, horseracing overtook football as my first love.

In the Ipswich team, Eric Gates loved a bet and was really into his racing, as were Paul Cooper and Kevin O'Callaghan. Gatesy was always single so had more time to study the form than most. Every day after training I'd find him in the changing room with a copy of the *Sporting Life*, analysing different horses' performances in previous races and generally keeping up with the news from the stables. Gatesy was a favourites man: he used to put them in doubles, trebles and accumulators, and he'd often win big.

Because of Ipswich's proximity to Newmarket there were a lot of people in the town with connections to horseracing and people would invite us to their yards. We'd be up at 5 a.m. and in Newmarket by six to watch trainers put their horses through their paces on the heath. There is no better sight in the world than a racehorse in full flight on the gallops. It was certainly better than spending the day in bed or playing snooker, which is what a lot of the other lads did in their downtime. And if we couldn't get down to Newmarket, we'd meet up for breakfast and spend the day in the bookies instead.

Sometimes an owner or his son would invite us to their house on race days, because they were as fascinated by footballers as we were by racing. I was just a kid from Glasgow, but rather than being intimidated by the incredible wealth on display, I was intrigued. Where did all their money come from? How could they afford to have houses in London and Barbados, as well as their

Left: In my playing days – rocking rather a lot more hair.

Right: Lacing up my boots for Tottenham Hotspur.

IPSWICH TOWN — UEFA CUP WINNERS 1980-81

Top: Our Ipswich Town team of 1980-81. A cracking bunch of lads.

Above: Celebrating scoring five goals against Southampton in 1982. A day I'll never forget.

Left: With Bobby Robson at a team dinner.

Above: My beloved Celtic were the first British team to be Champions of Europe in 1967. This commemorative shirt was one of many pieces auctioned at a charity dinner in London, shown here with Celtic legends Willie Wallace, Bertie Auld, Jim Craig, Bobby Lennox and John Clark (left to right).

Below: With my old pals at our annual Spurs Christmas lunch in London.

Above left: Then and now. Reminiscing at the talkSPORT studio.

Above right: With Mike 'Porky' Parry, my partner in crime for so many years.

Above: Cutting the cake for talkSPORT's twentieth anniversary. A special moment.

Left: Porky and me enjoying some light refreshment after the breakfast show.

Left: In the studio, enjoying a laugh with Niall Horan. We've had some cracking guests over the years, and there's never a dull moment.

Below: On the golf course with my good mates Ally McCoist and Ray Parlour.

Bottom left: The famous bottle of 2005 Petrus, which we eventually auctioned for the NHS. The winning bid was close to £25,000. Unbelievable!

Bottom right: Having a wee drink with Ray.

Above left: My first love. Here with Micky Quinn at Newmarket. Always a thrill to be at the races.

Above right: Wee Willie Carson trying to squeeze through a gap at Royal Ascot, my friend Charles Hayes on the left.

Left: Lining them up with Eddie Jordan. I do love a Guinness.

Top: Sharing fond memories with Sir Alex Ferguson.

Above: Dinner with a legend. Spending time with Sir Rod Stewart in Marbella.

Left: Turning sixty last year alongside my son-in-law, Dino Anastasiadis, turning forty. A special day.

What really matters. At Newmarket racecourse with my three daughters, Lucy, Michelle and Stephanie (**above**), and spending time with my granddaughter Olympia, on the Greek island of Paros (**left**).

Below: I'm a firm believer that life is for living, whether that's skiing in Meribel or sipping a cold beer by the Aegean Sea without a care in the world. Heaven.

own yard in Newmarket? I don't mind saying that I wanted a bit of it.

Charles St George was a flamboyant Lloyd's underwriter and racehorse owner who had houses in Mayfair and Newmarket, right next to Tattersalls sales ring – the premier auction house for racehorses in the UK and Ireland – in the centre of the town. The story goes that Charles settled Lester Piggott's unpaid bill when he got jailed for tax evasion, and his Newmarket pad, a magnificent Georgian edifice, was incredible. He'd invite us there for the Craven meeting in April and it would blow my mind. There were butlers serving champagne and canapés, and some of the greatest jockeys of the day – Piggott, Walter Swinburn, Steve Cauthen – would turn up. It was absolutely magical.

I realized these people were different from me, in that they had lots more money, spoke 'better' and were more sophisticated, but they were always lovely to me and I never felt uncomfortable in their presence. Another guy who looked after us Ipswich lads was the Greek shipping magnate and racehorse owner Marcos Lemos. Clive Brittain trained Marcos's horses at his Carlburg Stables in Newmarket, including Julio Mariner, which won the 1978 St Leger, and the filly Pebbles, which won the 1000 Guineas and Breeders' Cup Turf in 1984 and 1985 respectively. Marcos used to call Julio Mariner 'Paul', after Ipswich's centre-forward, and Pebbles used to be accompanied to meetings by a horse called Come On The Blues, who apparently had a calming influence.

In the end I became so infatuated with racing that during the summer, when we had a few weeks off from football, I'd be a regular at Clive Brittain's stables. I'd get there at 5.30 a.m. and ride out on one of his hacks to watch him train. Trainers like Clive and Henry Cecil, whom I also got to know well, just seemed so incredibly wise and I wanted to know as much as them.

I began to learn about the history of horseracing, starting with the three stallions that were imported from the Middle East in the seventeenth and eighteenth centuries – the Byerley Turk, the Darley Arabian and the Godolphin Arabian – and crossbred with native mares to create the Thoroughbred horses we see today (although this theory has been challenged of late). I learned about Charles II, who loved to race his hack Old Rowley on Newmarket Heath, which is why one of the racecourses is known as the Rowley Mile. I learned about the Craven Stakes, inaugurated in 1771 and named after the 6th Baron Craven, which many people, including me, regard as the start of the Flat season. I also loved the breeding aspect and enjoyed studying which bloodlines had produced winners in the Derby, Guineas, Oaks and St Leger.

Jockeys are some of my biggest heroes in sport, and none come greater than Lester Piggott. I've got a highlights video of Piggott at home and I've watched it so many times that it's almost worn out. What a maestro he was, an absolute genius. They called him 'The Long Fellow', because at 5ft 8in he was tall for a Flat jockey. That meant he had to sit further forward on the horse, to counter how long his legs were. Many jockeys tried to copy him and couldn't.

Lester had an aura about him, like all the great sports-people. Like Tiger Woods when he's practising on the range, Lester would draw a crowd in the parade ring. He was also ruthless, in that he always demanded the best horses and almost always got them, even if it meant other jockeys losing a ride on the day of a race. Whenever I spoke to him at the Craven meeting he was a lot smarter than his public image, with a wicked sense of humour.

The Americans didn't like him because they thought he was arrogant. In 1990, Lester came out of retirement and won the Breeders' Cup Mile in the US on Royal Academy at the age of fifty-four, forty-two years after he rode his first winner. It was a wonderful ride, with Royal Academy coming from seemingly nowhere to win by a neck. Afterwards, the American interviewer asked him when he thought he had the race in the bag and Lester replied, 'When Vincent O'Brien asked me to ride Royal Academy four weeks ago.'

As well as the owners, trainers and jockeys, there were all the other characters connected to the sport. My father-in-law, Roy Davis, had a building firm, loved his racing too, and would invite all sorts of people into his box on race days. That's where I got to know Charles Benson, who was a tipster for the *Daily Express*, a social-ite and an inveterate gambler. Charles was the right-hand man of Robert Sangster, the pools heir, businessman and owner whose horses won countless big races. I once attended a party at Robert's house in Moulton, just down the road from Newmarket, and it was as opulent a do as I can remember. Rod Stewart was also a guest, and when the party was over we shared a limousine to Robert's private marquee at the racecourse, then spent the rest of the day chatting about football. Charles was also a friend of Lord Lucan and the last person to see him alive before his disappearance in 1974.

The newspaper columnist Jeffrey Bernard once claimed that Charles had had a free holiday every month for the previous year, which I could well believe. By the 1980s he had a belly on him like you wouldn't believe. It was like an airbag had gone off under his shirt. So when he challenged me to a set of tennis at Jeremy Hindley's yard, I thought I'd annihilate him, because I was still playing football at the time and very fit. I was so confident of victory I had a bottle of champagne before the game. But he ended up beating me, in front of a big crowd of stable lads on horseback. I was gutted, until he informed me that he'd won Junior Wimbledon as a kid. I've no idea if he did or not (I've had a look and can't see his name on the honours list) but he was surprisingly good for a fat lad.

My favourite horse is Shergar, because when he won the Derby in 1981 I made a fortune, something like a grand. A few days before he was kidnapped in 1983 I had my picture taken with him at the Ballymany Stud in County Kildare. I've still got that photo up in my flat in London and whenever someone sees it they say, 'I wish they'd kidnapped you instead of the horse.' My favourite winner is Lester Piggott on Match Winner at Newmarket in 1982. I was a bit skint at the time, but various people told me to back it and it was too good to resist. I'm glad they've changed the whip rule because jockeys used to hit horses too much, but if Lester hadn't smacked Match Winner as much as he did that day, my bet wouldn't have come off. The horse was trained by Henry Cecil, and while the stewards' inquiry was taking place I remember Henry's wife Julie saying, 'That bastard Piggott has cost us.' But the result stood and I won a few grand, which was one of the most beautiful feelings I've ever experienced.

I backed another Henry Cecil-trained horse at Newmarket in 1989 – at 50-1. The horse was called Belmez and I naturally thought he had no chance in his first start, until I bumped into Julie Cecil and she advised me to back him. I had £50 on the nose and he beat another of Cecil's horses quite comfortably. The following year, Belmez won the King George at Ascot.

If I had to pick one bet I wish I'd never had, it would be Wayward Lad in the 1986 Cheltenham Gold Cup. People kept telling me that he wouldn't come up the hill, but I'd seen him finish third to Bregawn when Michael Dickinson trained the first five home in the same race three years earlier. So I had a grand each way at 10-1. Wayward Lad jumped the final fence in front, only for Dawn Run to get up and seal a famous win. Dawn Run's victory was as devastating as Match Winner's was beautiful.

A lot of footballers from my era were into their racing, probably because they had a lot of time on their hands and no computer games to play. Instead, they spent all their time in the bookies. When I was playing for Manchester United, I invited Bryan Robson along to York races one day. Bryan was a lovely down-to-earth guy with no airs or graces. He loved his football, loved his family, loved his mates and was just starting to get into his racing, because he'd become pals with a guy called Mike Dillon, who was a massive United fan and the PR man for Ladbrokes. The fact that I had a nice juicy tip clinched it for him.

Bryan got his driver to take us from Manchester to York in his beautiful Daimler, and I remember sitting in the back together and Bryan talking about how proud he was to have been made captain of his country and all the perks that came with the job. As we spoke, his agent was over in Germany, trying to sort him out with a nice big Mercedes.

My tip was for the third race, a fillies' handicap. My guy at Newmarket had told me to lump a maximum bet on a horse called Rye Tops. I thought that was a bit strange, because the whole point of a handicap race is that no horse is meant to have much of an advantage over the rest of the field. But my guy was adamant that this horse was a different class, except for one thing: when she hit the front, she stopped.

I thought he was having me on, so I said to him, 'Sorry, can you repeat that?'

'When she gets to the front, she sort of looks around and stops.'

'So why are you telling me to put on a maximum bet? Are you mad?'

'Don't worry, Alan, Pat Eddery will ride her.'

Pat Eddery had already been Champion Jockey a handful of times and my guy reckoned he knew this filly inside out.

'Pat will hold her and hold her, until the very last second, when she'll pounce and pass the post without having time to think about being ahead.'

I still wasn't entirely convinced.

After the second race, I managed to drag myself away from the hospitality tent and dashed down to the parade ring, where I found the guy who had given me the tip. He was looking a bit worried, so I said to him, 'Are you all right?'

'Well, we have a bit of a problem,' he told me.

'What problem?'

'There's been a crash on the A1 and Pat Eddery can't ride Rye Tops.'

'God. Is Pat all right?'

'He had nothing to do with it, but he can't get his car through.'

'So who's riding Rye Tops?'

'Brian Rouse.'

Brian Rouse was a good jockey, just not as good as Pat Eddery. So I said, 'Shall I halve my bet then?'

'No, no, no. Double it.'

'What do you mean, double it?'

'Brian Rouse exercises Rye Tops in the morning at Newmarket. He also knows that when she hits the front, she looks around and stops.'

'I'm not happy about this . . .'

I told Bryan what had happened and that I was thinking about halving my bet, and he persuaded me to hold my nerve. So we both smashed big bets on Rye Tops – a couple of grand each way, which was a lot of money in 1985, and still is – and went off to watch the race, me with a bad feeling in my bones.

Inside the final furlong there were three horses out in front and Rye Tops was coming up on the rails, looking for room. And with about half a furlong to go, a gap opened up. Rye Tops burst through it and went half a length clear. Then a length. Then two lengths. But then what my guy said would happen started happening. The field started coming back at her and the gap was shortening all the time – back to a length, back to half a length – and it ended up as a bunch finish, just as a handicap should.

For a moment we didn't know if she'd held on or not. And I don't mind admitting that I was shitting myself, because I'd emptied my pockets. But the replays showed that she'd hung on to win by a short head and the big tip had come off. That was one of my most frightening experiences at a racecourse, but also one of the most euphoric.

Me and Bryan had also tipped off some of our mates, and we all met up in the champagne bar afterwards. And while we were celebrating, we got chatting to the trainer Denys Smith, who was from Bryan's part of the world, County Durham. Denys gave us another tip for the last race, we all piled on that, and it came in as well.

That was some evening, and me and Bryan were

among the last to leave the course. We fell into the waiting Daimler, opened up another bottle of champagne, and I almost forgot about the Sainsbury's bag with £27,000 in it (to put that into perspective, United were paying me around a grand and a half a week at the time). Never mind a Sainsbury's bag, I should have had a wheelbarrow. And Bryan hadn't done badly either.

As we were nearing Manchester, I said to Bryan, 'I've got a great idea.'

'What?'

'Well, you're buying a new Merc. So why don't I have your Daimler and you can have this cash?'

'What?'

'Please, Bryan. I can't take this home. The wife will kill me.'

You might be asking why my wife wouldn't have been thrilled with me winning £27,000. Because she knew that if I could win £27,000 that easily, I could also lose it that easily. Eventually, Bryan realized that my idea would also get him out of a sticky situation, because while he hadn't won as much as me, he had still won a lot. So the plan was that Bryan would tell his wife he'd sold me his Daimler. Then, when the Mercedes arrived, he'd drop the Daimler at mine, I'd give him the money I'd won and he'd deposit it in his bank. Considering how pissed we were, it was quite a cunning proposition.

Two days later I phoned up a pal who flew shuttles from Manchester to Edinburgh and Belfast and said, 'Right, me and you are going to Newmarket for two days. I'll pay you cash for the flight and I'll also pay for everything once we're there.' So on the Friday morning, the two of us set off in his plane and we had a great couple of days. The only problem being, we didn't have any luck.

Back in Manchester, Bryan phoned me on the Sunday morning and said, 'Brilliant news. I've got the Merc and the Daimler is yours.' To which I replied, 'Sorry, Bryan, I'm skint. Bad day at Newmarket, I did the lot.' And I wasn't lying. I somehow managed to blow £27,000 in two days. Ridiculous.

I can't say it bothered me too much because I was very easy come, easy go in those days. But I'd left Bryan in a bit of a spot: he now had to explain to his wife why he had been paid thousands of pounds in cash for the Daimler but it was still on the drive next to his brand-new Mercedes. I must admit I found the whole situation hilarious, and Bryan saw the funny side too, at least after he'd managed to offload the Daimler to some car dealer he knew.

I wouldn't want you to get the idea that I often jet up and down the country solely to attend the races, but another of my biggest betting coups did involve a plane trip and two meetings on the same day, 135 miles apart. First, I travelled to Newbury, armed with what I thought was an exclusive tip on a filly. Because I thought this tip was so exclusive and potentially very lucrative, I kept myself to myself before the race, until I was spotted by my pal Alan Ball. The first thing Bally said to me was, 'You're here for that filly, aren't you? Miss Bagatelle?'

We were soon joined by Mick Channon, and they

proceeded to tell me about another horse that might pose a danger to Miss Bagatelle. Having been utterly convinced that Miss Bagatelle was going to walk it, I was now torn, because I knew how much they both knew about horses, Mick in particular.

Only when they were putting the horses in the stalls did I finally make my mind up, sticking two grand on Miss Bagatelle and two grand on Bally and Channon's tip, both on the nose. Thank God I bumped into those two. Miss Bagatelle faded early and their tip won the race at 4-1, meaning that instead of losing four grand, I now had eight grand to play with for the rest of the day.

Shortly after that I bumped into Willie Carson's pilot and cadged a lift to Newmarket for the evening meeting. But before the flight, Willie had one more race, which his pilot was convinced he'd win. So I put a couple of hundred quid on him, watched him romp home, and a few minutes later we were sitting on his plane. En route to Newmarket, the pilot gave me another tip, a horse called Sheriff's Star. But when we landed I asked a bookie about it and he told me it was odds-on favourite, so I decided it wasn't worth backing.

I headed to the drinks tent, where people kept asking me who I fancied in the next race. I told them I expected Sheriff's Star to win but that it wasn't a very attractive price. Not only that, it was a twenty-seven-runner maiden race, so I told them I thought it was a lottery. Because I didn't have a bet on it I didn't take any notice of the race. But after the noise had died down, people were all over me, shaking my hand, showering me with kisses, thrusting glasses of champagne into my hand. It was only when I looked up at the TV that I understood why: Sheriff's Star had won, at 33-1. That was a blow.

When I looked at the full list of runners, I realized what must have happened: the favourite was called something like Shareef Afar, so the bookie I spoke to must have misheard me. I couldn't really blame him because I had drunk an awful lot of champagne that day.

In the early 2000s, me and a couple of mates bought a beautiful chestnut horse called Indian Haven. It is well known that horses aren't cheap, so when my wife found out, she went ballistic. His first race as a two-year-old was at Yarmouth, and because my trainer Paul D'Arcy thought he was such a special horse, I stuck two grand on him. I was going on holiday two days later so really shouldn't have been risking that kind of money. To my immense relief, Indian Haven won by a couple of lengths. But when I went to collect my money, the bookie said, 'I don't think so, you backed the favourite.' I told him I'd said Indian Haven, and the guy next to me backed me up. But the bookie wasn't having it, so in the end I had to get the adjudicator from the betting ring and he told the bookie to pay me out. That was a heart-stopping moment. Had he not sided with me, it would have been a very frugal holiday indeed.

Indian Haven was moved up in class and was unlucky not to win any of his next three races, before trailing in last in the Dewhurst Stakes at Newmarket. And despite

Johnny Murtagh, who rode him in his third race, at Doncaster, insisting that Indian Haven would do better on softer ground, we decided to sell him. Shortly after that I was on a plane headed for the Dubai World Cup and got chatting to a top bloodstock agent called Charlie Gordon-Watson. When I told him we'd sold Indian Haven, Charlie said, 'I wouldn't have done that, he's probably just been a bit unlucky.'

Charlie and Johnny Murtagh were right. The following year Indian Haven finished fourteenth in the 2000 Guineas, but probably would have been placed if he hadn't been trapped against the rail. And in the Irish 2000 Guineas, on soft ground at the Curragh, he won comfortably by a length. Suddenly, Indian Haven was worth a few million quid. We made something like £40,000 when we sold him, but we shouldn't have blinked.

In 2003, I set up the Alan Brazil Racing Club. I pumped in a lot of my own money and, once again, my wife thought I'd lost my mind. But that's just me – I always dive right in. We made it cheap to join, about £160, and we had a great time for a while. We'd take members to watch the horses on the gallops and race all over the country. We'd all have a good drink and I'd take them into the ring to meet the jockeys. I absolutely loved it, as did the members.

The mistake we made was getting too carried away too soon. Instead of sticking with two or three horses, we quickly ended up with about twenty. It took up so much of my time, and when we hit a run of bad luck, people stopped joining and we started running out of money. I'd love to do it again, but differently. To have a chance of winning, you have to charge members a lot more than £160 to join. That's the only way you can make it work, because horses burn through cash at an alarming rate. It costs about £30,000 a year to keep one, and champs and duds all eat the same amount. Racing can certainly cost you a lot of money, because there are a lot of very wealthy people to keep up with, but I've never regretted getting involved. There have been a few lows, but it's mainly been exhilarating.

8

Bread and Butter

Over the years at talkSPORT I've had more co-presenters than most people have had hot dinners. In 2004, Porky stepped aside after having a few problems with his health. He says he had something wrong with his heart, but I reckon it was to do with his liver (don't worry, he'd find that funny). Porky's still around the station and pops up on various shows, like *Hawksbee and Jacobs*, and we always try to have a drink whenever he's in town. Were it not for his heart problems, we could be celebrating twenty years together on the breakfast show. Frightening thought!

Porky was replaced by Graham 'Beeky' Beecroft. I loved Beeky, because he was such a nice, placid guy. In fact, Beeky was almost too nice: it would take quite a lot to rile him. After Beeky, ex-England cricketer Ronnie Irani was my sidekick for six years, and he was a great lad as well. But when the listening numbers dropped a wee bit in 2013, the bosses decided he had to go.

Broadcasting is brutal like that: one minute you're flying high, the next you're out of a job and have nothing on the horizon. But as heartbroken as Ronnie was, it was also an opportunity to freshen things up. I suggested we have a different co-presenter every day of the week, to keep things lively, and it worked, because we soon clawed those lost listeners back.

Among my rotating cast of sidekicks have been former England manager Sam Allardyce, former Liverpool and Wales striker Dean Saunders, former Spurs and France winger David Ginola, former Newcastle striker and racehorse trainer Micky Quinn, former England rugby international Brian Moore, veteran football manager Neil Warnock, former England cricketer Dominic Cork and, of course, my great pals Ally McCoist and Ray Parlour.

Having a rolling roster of co-presenters also means it's easier to persuade on to the air bigger names who would never agree to present five shows a week. That's how we managed to get people like England Rugby World Cup winner Lawrence Dallaglio and Olympic cycling legend Sir Bradley Wiggins, as well as controversial footballer Joey Barton, who is never afraid to speak his mind.

Because people know I like a night out and sound like I'm chatting to my mates down the pub, they think what I do is easy. When I'm on with Parlour or McCoist there is certainly plenty of natural banter and piss-taking. That's why I look forward to working with them so much.

With McCoist, I suddenly revert to being a Glaswegian again and words pop into my head that I haven't used since leaving Scotland in 1975. I remember playing against McCoist when he was a boy at Sunderland. Bobby Robson said, 'Keep an eye on this Scottish kid, he's meant to be red hot.' He wasn't that day, but he went on to be one of Scotland's greatest strikers. I have a lot of respect for him, as a footballer and a broadcaster. We get on like a house on fire and broadcasting with him is easy. He's got great patter, we're both bubbly characters, and people always say that we've got something special as a double act. We can say things to each other that we might not be able to say to anyone else. Some of the banter might seem near the knuckle, but it will never go too far, because we trust each other.

But while I take it as a compliment that people think it sounds like we're propping up a bar, it's a little bit more sophisticated than that. Four hours is a long time to fill every morning so there has to be some structure and discipline to go with the laughing and joking. For example, it's not a good idea to be giggling when you throw to the news, because the lead story might be particularly horrible. That might sound basic, but try remembering that every time, day in, day out. Entertainment is about conjuring the right mix of fun and professionalism. And, believe it or not, I take what I do seriously.

Until talkSPORT was bought by News Corp in 2016 I didn't think we had anything like as much advertising as we should have had. That made me angry. And if I'm not happy with the way someone has spoken to me, we haven't got enough staff, or the guests aren't good enough, I can get annoyed and a bit snappy. You'd think that having done the show for twenty years I'd have a say in my guests, but most mornings I turn up, someone tells me who's going to be on and I just have to get on with it. I make requests, but that doesn't mean we'll get them. That irritates me, because we're a major player on the landscape, too big a show to cock up, and we should have the very best.

Twenty years after doing my first breakfast show, people still wonder if I'm going to turn up of a morning. Some of that is down to the fact that after the Cheltenham sacking in 2004, Kelvin MacKenzie decided to make a big thing of my drinking and even came up with a slogan: 'Alan Brazil has just left the pub.' People I've worked with are always being asked, 'How does Alan Brazil do what he does? Surely he's not drinking every day like he says he is?' And when they say that I am, they're astonished. Some people might think I'm unprofessional. But my record over twenty years is pretty good, let me tell you.

There have been times when I've had to phone in the middle of the night and tell them I can't make it in, and they've been fine about it. Listeners automatically think I've not turned up because I've been on the piss. I understand that, because a lot of my stories are about days and nights out drinking. I can't have it both ways. But that's usually not the case.

For example, at the 2020 Cheltenham Festival, which probably shouldn't have taken place because of coronavirus, I was flying all week and then fell out of bed on the Thursday night, smashing my back and breaking the top of my thumb. Luckily my wife was with me. I immediately phoned work and told them I couldn't move. I didn't want to miss the show or the Gold Cup because I like to finish Cheltenham off in style, but there wasn't much I could do about it. There have also been times when I've gone on air when I shouldn't have. When former Aston Villa goalkeeper Mark Bosnich was over from Australia, he was invited to co-present the show with me. But when I turned up at the offices I was in pieces because I'd eaten some dodgy seafood the night before. If Mark hadn't been in town I wouldn't have worked that day. And while the show wasn't the best, I soldiered on and we got it done.

Broadcasting is similar to being a professional footballer. When you're at the top of your game, you're scoring goals and the money is rolling in, you feel invincible. And when the radio show is pulling in record audiences, a new sponsor has come on board and you're getting great guests on, you feel the same. But you're not always flying. Doing what I've done for so long is not natural. I'd like to see my critics try to do what I've done for two decades: get up in the middle of the night Monday to Friday, get to the studio and talk enthusiastically for four hours with no music to break things up. That's why so many people in the industry end up dabbling in drugs to keep them going.

Inevitably there are days when I'm not really feeling in the mood. Sometimes I'll have to talk about mates who have died. That was the case with Ray Wilkins, whose death from a cardiac arrest in 2018 absolutely gutted me, and Alan Ball, another great football man who passed away suddenly in 2007. Occasionally I'll actually be on air when I hear bad news. Following the Champions League semi-final second leg between Liverpool and Chelsea in 2007, a helicopter crashed after leaving John Lennon Airport. While I was presenting the show the following morning, news came through that my mate Phillip Carter, a Chelsea vice-president, had been on board, along with his teenage son. Both were dead. Moments like that are very challenging. But as long as that red light is on, you just have to hold it together. You don't really have a choice, because it's not about you. Part of the skill of being a radio presenter is to be upbeat and positive, even if you don't feel great. It's the same as having to perform as a footballer despite carrying a niggling injury. I'm essentially an entertainer, trying to give people a lift at the start of a new day.

And if giving people a lift means getting out of the studio and taking a risk, I'm happy to do it. In 2004, I was sitting at the bar in the Colony Club casino in Mayfair when I happened to see a news report on the TV behind the bar. It was about the cancellation of a British Airways flight from Heathrow to Washington, because of rumours that it was a terrorist target. This flight had been cancelled for three consecutive days because no one would get on it, so I suddenly had a brainwave. I phoned Porky and said, 'I'm sick of these terrorists stopping people from going about their normal lives. We're going to do something about it. The next time that flight takes to the skies, we'll be on it. And when it lands, we're going to do the show from Washington.'

We contacted BA, told them our plan, and they were delighted. The officials at the US Embassy in London were baffled, to put it mildly, that we were so determined to fly to Washington on that particular plane, but after some heavy grilling they gave us both visas.

A couple of days later we were sitting in BA's first-class lounge at Heathrow waiting to board the first flight to Washington for five days. On the way to the gate, BA staff and other passengers gave us a round of applause. We almost had the plane to ourselves – there must have been about half a dozen people on it. Take-off was delayed for about three hours because of all the extra security procedures, so by the time the plane was in the air, Porky and I had drunk them out of champagne.

I never once felt unsafe on the flight (although that might have had something to do with the amount of booze we got through) and we were brilliantly looked after by the cabin crew. Porky even interviewed a few of them, as well as the captain after landing. At Dulles International Airport we were greeted by a limousine driver who must have been 6ft 7in, holding a giant white board with our names on it. He called himself 'Mr Washington', in that he knew everything there was to know about the city.

After dropping off our bags at the hotel, Mr Washington ferried us straight to a Celtic supporters club (there are hundreds of Celtic supporters clubs all over the world, from Abu Dhabi to Prague to Hong Kong), where we spent the evening sinking pints of the black stuff and singing Irish songs.

I only managed to get a couple of hours' sleep before waking up at some ungodly hour and trudging through snow to the studio. And I have to admit, when I was sat there with the headphones on waiting for the light to go on, I wasn't exactly brimming with inspiration. Porky, meanwhile, looked like he might die. But as soon as that light went on and a cacophony of noise flooded my cans, I was back in the room. We did a brilliant show that day, despite the combination of jetlag, Guinness and lack of sleep. I don't know whether that was down to adrenalin or knowing I had a responsibility to entertain. I suspect a combination of the two, because what I do know is this: it doesn't matter how I'm feeling, what matters is making other people feel good.

I love that Muhammad Ali quote, when he was asked if he was any good at golf: 'I'm the best. I just haven't played yet.' I'm not saying I'm the best broadcaster in the world by any means, but until you try something, you won't find out if you can do it or not. I had a natural aptitude for radio broadcasting, but I had to learn. And when you try hard at something, you will get better at it. And the fact that my breakfast show has consistently had 1.5 million listeners means I must do it better than most.

While I'm on the subject of ratings, I've always been convinced it's probably nearer to three million listeners, because I've never met anyone who fills in these diaries the researchers use to calculate the figures. I also get emails, texts and tweets from all over the world – South America, Kazakhstan, the Far East, Africa, even Papua New Guinea. When I presented the show from the Pig and Whistle pub in Brisbane during the 2017/18 Ashes series, it wasn't just members of the Barmy Army that knew me, it was Aussies as well. On top of that, I'm always being told, 'I love your show on 5 Live, Alan!'

Sometimes, youngsters will ask me for advice on how

to break into radio or how to improve as a broadcaster. I'll give them a few tips, stuff like always staying on top of the news and reading about anything and everything, and sometimes I'll invite them into the talkSPORT studios to see how a big commercial radio station is run. But my main advice is to graft and not see any job as beneath you. If you want to be a broadcaster or a producer or a researcher you might have to start off making the tea and running errands. Then, once you've got a foot in the door, you might impress the right people and start rising up the ranks. There are lots of diamonds out there, don't worry about that, but those who get on in the industry are those who work the hardest.

To be successful at anything, you've also got to believe in yourself. When I've got a mic in my hand I have complete belief, whereas when I played football my confidence wasn't always 100 per cent. When I was on my game, especially in my Ipswich days, I feared no one. If I was through on goal, I didn't even think about missing. It was more a case of 'Where am I going to put it? To his left? To his right? Underneath him? Over his head?' But there were other times when I wasn't quite right. When I moved to a new club, I sometimes tried too hard and did things to try to please the crowd which didn't really suit me. But I never had the same problems when it came to broadcasting. When you stick to your strengths, the confidence naturally follows. And the more confident you become, the more your talent blossoms.

The laid-back approach works for me but fills some of my co-presenters with dread. McCoist often tells the story of his first day working alongside me. He was very excited and slightly nervous so turned up an hour early, to make sure he was properly prepared. But at about 5.50, with just ten minutes to go until the start of the show, I still hadn't turned up and Ally was getting twitchy, wondering if he'd have to present his first show on his own. When the producer Dave Richards walked past, Ally said to him, 'What time do we start worrying?' Dave replied, 'If he hasn't turned up by the end of the six o'clock news.' Ally claims I walked into the studio with two minutes to spare, telling him not to panic. He's exaggerating wildly, because it was more like three.

After doing it for so long I've got it down to a fine art: rock up to the offices at 5.54, in the studio by 5.57, pick up a newspaper, skim-read the top three stories, the red light goes on, off we go. It might be hair-raising for some of my co-presenters, but I'm not worried, because the likes of McCoist and Parlour are never short of a few words. If I'm going to be really delayed, I'll call ahead and let them know. But the worst that usually happens is my co-presenter has to fill in until the first travel break at 6.13. And once we're on air my relaxed approach rubs off on my co-presenters. We'll be munching on biscuits while the news is on and have the after-show festivities all organized by eight o'clock.

The more comfortable you are in that environment, the more you can be yourself, the more opinionated you can be, and the more comfortable your audience will be, as if they're sitting in a pub with you. Sometimes my listeners have spent too much time in a real pub. My show doesn't rely on callers like other shows, but I like to take the odd call from a fan who is passionate about football and their team. But you've got to be careful, because if you give a numptie too much airtime, people will switch off. The easiest way to get rid of a rambling drunk (and we do get them, even at 7 a.m.) is to say, 'Sorry, it's not the greatest of lines, I appreciate your call but we'll have to leave it there.' I'm never nasty, because you don't know what's going on in these people's lives. I just let them say their piece, make a quick call, and move on.

Of course, there's a fine line between feeling comfortable and becoming blasé. And the problem with live radio is that if you put your foot in it, it will be remembered for ever. That's why so many radio broadcasters have bitten the dust down the years. One morning we had the TV critic Garry Bushell on, despite the fact that I don't watch much telly. Garry was chatting away to Porky and I wasn't really listening, until I heard Garry mention a BAFTA tribute to Bob Monkhouse. I said I'd once seen Bob do stand-up and how surprisingly blue he'd been, followed by the line that makes me cringe to this day: 'Garry, how about Bob's health now?'

There was a short pause before Garry replied, in a hushed voice, 'He died at Christmas.'

Porky, who was shaking his head and had steam coming out of his ears, tried to patch things up before I followed up with, 'I heard two different versions . . .'

Porky still says to me, 'How can there be two different versions?'

They still play that clip on talkSPORT and I still get slaughtered, but what people have to remember is that when you do a show for twenty years, you're going to make the odd innocent mistake. I wasn't being disrespectful to Bob Monkhouse, I just didn't know he'd died.

Then there was the time the actor John Thaw passed away. I said, 'I was sad to hear yesterday about the death of Inspector Morse, TV's John Shaw.'

Poor old Porky said, 'John Thaw, Alan.'

And I replied, 'Do you know, I've been doing that all morning. John, if you're listening, sorry, mate.'

But far worse was the Hansie Cronje gaffe, which I still have to listen to through my fingers. It happened during the Cricket World Cup in South Africa in 2003, when I was chatting to our reporter Neil Manthorp. I've got to know plenty of cricketers through talkSPORT, great guys like Steve Harmison, Ronnie Irani and Dominic Cork, and I really take an interest in cricket nowadays. But back in 2003, it wasn't really my game. So, once again, I was half listening to Neil when I should have been giving him my full attention. He started going on about all the great players he'd been doing commentary with and I suddenly blurted out, 'Will Hansie be joining you?'

The line went quiet for a couple of seconds, which is never a good thing on radio, before eventually Neil replied, 'Hansie Cronje?'

'Yeah, will he not be popping in?'

There was another pause, before Neil said, 'Hansie died in a plane crash.'

And all I could say was, 'Oh, sorry, I must have been on holiday.'

I thought, 'Holy shit, I've done it again . . .'

When I first took the breakfast job, I thought I'd just be talking about sport. But I soon realized that I was expected to talk about pretty much anything, from politics to terrorist attacks to celebrity gossip. I don't mind admitting that I'm not big on research, but I read a lot of magazines and have a very good memory, which is a massive help in the job. People tell me how daunted they'd be, having to talk almost non-stop for four hours a day. But I've never run out of things to say and I never will.

Every Wednesday I'll pick up a random magazine and read it from cover to cover, and there will always be something in there that I'll be able to use on the radio. A few months ago we were talking about Whitby in Yorkshire and I mentioned that Captain Cook was an apprentice in the town and that Bram Stoker was staying there when he got his inspiration for *Dracula*. My fellow presenters looked at me like I was mad, but I read that in *Country Life*. I've worked with people who turn up an hour early and read every newspaper front to back. When Eamonn Holmes sat in for me a few times, he'd turn up at 4.30. I thought his missus must have locked him out of his house. But, as I've said, that's not my style. We've got a team who briefly fill me in on what's happening in the world, but most of what I talk about just comes to me naturally.

When we had the actor Dan Aykroyd on, I thought we were going to talk about his film career – *The Blues Brothers, Trading Places, Ghostbusters* – but he wanted to talk about UFOs instead. Funnily enough, in Rendlesham Forest, which is near where I live, there were some alleged UFO sightings in the early 1980s, so I had a bit of knowledge of the subject. Some of the punters didn't enjoy it – they emailed to tell us, which they're perfectly entitled to do – but I could have chatted to Dan about UFOs for the whole four hours.

Dan also brought two bottles of vodka with him, a big one and a small one, because he owns his own company, Crystal Head Vodka. The bottles are in the shape of skulls, and he'd done a deal with the Rolling Stones to make it the official spirit of their fiftieth anniversary 2013 tour. Afterwards, Ronnie Irani asked him to sign a bottle. When Dan grabbed the big one and was about to put felt-tip to glass, I said, 'It's for Alan – A-L-A-N.' So I ended up taking home a bottle that was as big as my head and Ronnie ended up with one the size of his fist.

During the coronavirus lockdown I had Bill Oddie on, talking about birds. I rattled off the names of a few that come into my garden and he seemed genuinely surprised. So many broadcasters don't even pretend to be into what their guests are into, so when you are, they're often quite chuffed. As well as watching and feeding birds, I read about them in *Country Life*, usually in the garden with a glass of wine. That magazine is like my *Encyclopaedia Britannica*.

But while I knew who Bill Oddie was and had a bit of

knowledge of birds, I often have people on I've never heard of. In those cases you've just got to be smart, ask the right questions and let them reveal themselves. Confidence and sharpness can paper over cracks in knowledge. And if I still don't know what they're talking about, I'll throw to Ally McCoist!

I recently worked out that I must have spoken to something like ten thousand guests over twenty years, and I've had so many big stars on that I've lost track of them. More recently, a couple of my favourites have been Martin Compston, who starred in *Line of Duty* and also played a few games for Greenock Morton in the Scottish League, and Stephen Graham. Stephen has starred in *This Is England*, *Gangs of New York*, *The Irishman*, *Line of Duty* and *Boardwalk Empire*, in which he played Al Capone (I love anything to do with gangsters). You don't get much bigger than Stephen in terms of British actors. He's an absolute gem who loves chatting about the movies and could talk about his beloved Liverpool for hours on end.

I think I look up to actors more than I do footballers, because when I was growing up, becoming an actor seemed so fantastical, whereas I always thought I could become a footballer. I'd watch TV or go to the pictures and think, 'How on earth did they manage to get where they have?' Now I know that many actors come from similarly humble backgrounds to footballers.

Ray Winstone used to come on the show quite a bit, and he's another working-class boy who has done very well for himself. I also love a good British gangster movie (*Layer Cake*, with Daniel Craig and a young Tom Hardy, is maybe my favourite) and Ray has been in some classics. One of Ray's old mates, a commercial director called Gary Pettit, works in my building and we sometimes meet up for lunch in the City. Those days can get quite heavy, but thankfully Ray, who I love to bits, always wants to get back to Essex at some point, which means I can get back to Canary Wharf and get my head down. We've also had my fellow Glaswegian Robert Carlyle on, he of *The Full Monty* and *Trainspotting*; Jason Isaacs, who has played lots of memorable villains, including the horrendous English officer in *The Patriot* and Lucius Malfoy in the Harry Potter film series; and Cillian Murphy from *Peaky Blinders*.

When *Peaky Blinders* first came out I absolutely loved it and kept going on about it on the show. So eventually we got the show's creator Steven Knight on and we've since become good friends. He sends *Peaky Blinders* newsboy hats to the studio, and when a new series is about to come out and they have a premiere for cast and friends he always invites me along. On top of that, he once signed some handwritten scripts and donated them as an auction prize for a Celtic FC Foundation event.

Steven's a big Birmingham City fan and the inspiration for *Peaky Blinders* came from his family, so it was something he was dreaming about creating for years. At one of our lunches we got chatting about the gangsters in Glasgow and I suggested a few books for him to read for research, including *No Mean City* by H. Kingsley

Long, about the razor gangs of the Gorbals that my dad used to tell me about, and *Cut and Run* by Bill McGhee, about the seedy side of life in the Glasgow slums. I'm not saying I had anything to do with it, but Steven wrote some Glaswegian gangsters, the Billy Boys, into the next series.

To be honest, though, I don't watch a great deal of TV now. The occasional series will suck me in, like *Peaky Blinders* or *The Sopranos*, which I absolutely adored. But I'm more likely to watch old war movies. I can watch two or three in a row, especially anything about Vietnam – *Platoon*, *The Deer Hunter*, Mel Gibson's *We Were Soldiers*.

When Roger Moore was on the show, I couldn't quite understand why. He was doing a one-man tour at the time (or, as he called it, 'a one-and-a-half-man show', because he needed someone else on stage with him to jog his memory) and shooting off to Norwich straight from the talkSPORT offices. Now, there's obviously nothing wrong with coming on talkSPORT or with the beautiful city of Norwich (apart from its football team), but I just couldn't get my head around why he was still darting all over the country well into his eighties. It couldn't have been for the money, so maybe he just knew his time was running out and wanted to make the most of it. I'd always loved Roger in whatever he was in, whether it was James Bond, *The Saint* or *The Persuaders*, so I felt humbled chatting away to him. He was lovely, an absolute gentleman.

During our chat I reminded Roger about the time I

bumped into him on the dance floor at the Red Cross Ball in Monaco, sometime in the early 1990s. Strangely, he didn't remember. The Red Cross Ball is a lavish black-tie charity fundraiser attended by the rich and famous, with music, dancing, feasting and copious amounts of champagne. The year I attended, French crooner Charles Aznavour was the compère and the music was provided by Kid Creole and the Coconuts and Shirley Bassey, who lived around the corner from Roger in Monte Carlo. I was on a table with my old Spurs team-mate Paul Miller, who was working for a big bank at the time, and we spent most of the evening with our jaws on the floor, utterly awestruck by the glitz and glamour on show.

After an incredible fireworks display, Paul's boss wandered over and said, 'Sorry, I've got to go, I've got a new baby at home. Just make sure you sign for the bill.' Before Paul could say anything, his boss had disappeared. Our table was covered in magnums of Dom Pérignon, so Paul was terrified he was going to get cleaned out. We spent the next hour finishing off the dregs, like a couple of old boys in a Glasgow pub, before a waiter came over and said, 'Gentlemen, would you like another magnum?'

There was a pause, before Paul said, 'My boss has gone to bed and asked me to sort the bill. But I'm not sure my card can handle it.'

The waiter broke into a smile and replied, 'Don't worry about that, sir. You only have to sign for the bill, you don't have to pay for it. You can drink what you like.'

Me and Paul looked at each other, before I said, 'Two more magnums of Dom Pérignon, please.' We were the last two to leave.

One of my favourite footballing guests was Wayne Rooney, believe it or not. Before I do a big interview with anyone I always ask if there's anything they don't want to talk about, because I don't want to piss them off and make them clam up. But when I asked Wayne, he said I could ask him what I liked.

People love to have a go at Wayne and think he's thick. What a load of nonsense. He was such a warm, lovely guy and gave me three times as much time as we'd originally agreed. His intelligence really shone through when he was talking about football and some of the great goals he scored for Everton, Manchester United and England. I've always admired him for joining United from Everton, because it was a bold move for a little teenage Scouser. But what I like most about Wayne is that he's still playing football when he could have his feet up and be counting his millions. He had a crack in America playing for DC United and now he's banging them in for Derby, for whom he's player-coach, in the Championship. That tells me he loves the game and not just the riches it's brought him.

David Beckham is similar. For years he was mocked for being stupid and more interested in money than football. But he was a model professional, someone who took the game deadly seriously but was smart enough to make plenty of money on the side and leave a lasting legacy. He's fighting tooth and nail to get that stadium complex built over in Miami and I think he'll get it over the line. He could have walked away from that project, because it's been a lot of hassle for him and has been dragging on for years. But he's sticking with it because he's such a determined character and, like Wayne, he's still in love with the game. Being a big celebrity who spends his life mixing with seriously famous people can go to a man's head. But when I interviewed David he was as good as gold, down to earth and a pleasure to deal with.

I've never been starstruck, but I am in awe of boxers. I've had a few heavyweight greats on the show, including George Foreman in the studio and Mike Tyson on the phone. One of my favourite interviews was Tyson Fury. He turned up looking a million dollars, as if he'd come directly from Savile Row. Apart from his height, he didn't look like a heavyweight boxer. He certainly didn't turn up with an entourage, like some of them do. He was just very down to earth.

Tyson is obviously a complicated man but fascinating with it, and he bared his soul for the best part of an hour. He spoke about his struggles with depression, his split personality, and how he'd been putting on an act for most of his boxing career. The story about him wanting to drive his car into a tree, in order to end it all, was quite chilling. While he spoke, he never stopped looking me straight in the eye. He was just so matter of fact about such harrowing things. Sometimes you come off air and just know you've been part of something special. After Tyson had left the studio, Ally McCoist looked at me, shook his head, puffed out his cheeks and said, 'Wow, that was magic.'

As much as I love Tyson Fury, the best British heavyweight I've ever seen was Lennox Lewis. People say he's Canadian, but that's bollocks. He was born in Britain and boxed under the British flag, and that's enough for me. The first time I saw Lennox I was in Roger Moore's restaurant Hush in Mayfair, which is run by his son Geoffrey. Lennox walked in with an entourage of eight or nine people and I couldn't believe the size of him; he was absolutely massive. But when he came into the studio a few years ago he was about half as big. Like a lot of boxers, especially heavyweights, Lennox put on a bit of a persona while he was fighting. But he's a real gentleman and a great talker. We chatted about his fights against Mike Tyson and Evander Holyfield and about Tyson Fury and Anthony Joshua, and I was just so at ease in his company. He was so lovely, I felt like saying to him, 'Come on, let's go and have a few pints.'

Other times, the guests are a bit more serious. The newsreader Trevor McDonald was fascinating and another absolute gentleman. He chatted about visiting Saddam Hussein at his palace in Baghdad and being the first journalist to interview Nelson Mandela after his release from prison. How often do you get to meet people who have been in the company of such great figures, good and bad? I could have chatted to Trevor for hours.

When America and Britain invaded Afghanistan and Iraq in 2001 and 2003 respectively, we had military guys coming on the show: generals, analysts and journalists. When grave things like that happen I have an extra responsibility to get things right, so I'd be up watching CNN until the early hours to make sure I knew what was going on. But that's when the back-up team comes into its own. They'll be up all night booking guests and finding out exactly what's going on before laying it on a plate for me when I arrive in the morning, so that I know the right questions to ask and don't end up looking silly. Those guys and girls are the unsung heroes of the show. They work crazy hours and don't get paid a huge amount of money, which annoys me. Without them I wouldn't have the great guests I do and the knowledge and figures to be able to converse with them.

Genuine gaffes aside, sometimes I'll say something I really mean that upsets people. One morning I thought my wife had told me that the singer Robbie Williams had taken his own life. After I worked out she was actually talking about the comedian Robin Williams, I expressed my relief. Not because I had anything against Robin, but because I didn't really know much about him, whereas I really liked Robbie. Anyway, when I relayed this story on the show, it sounded a bit callous. And when I went on to say that I didn't have much sympathy for Robin Williams, and that I was angry that he'd caused his loved ones so much pain and had left them to clear up the mess, it didn't go down well. talkSPORT was inundated with complaints and I got slaughtered on social media. I even ended up having a row with talkSPORT colleague

Stan Collymore on Twitter. But he had his opinions and I was entitled to mine.

Since I started doing the show, the world has become far more politically correct. For years hardly anyone batted an eyelid at the things I said but now that's changed completely. I have to be a lot more careful about what I say because people are just waiting for me to slip up. And if I do slip up, people claim to be very angry and desperately try to get me sacked. Nowadays a live radio broadcaster is never far from disaster, because rules change without you getting the memo and you never know who you might upset.

When I was a kid, I'd often hear people say, 'Did you get a bird last night?' But if I used that phrase now, they'd be on me like a ton of bricks. I once got into trouble for referring to Rangers supporters as 'huns', not realizing that that term was now considered to be highly offensive. When I was growing up in Glasgow, Rangers fans called Celtic fans Fenians and we called them huns, that's how it was. If we were beating Rangers and their fans started leaving before the final whistle, we'd all put our hands in the air and sing 'Go home you huns, go home you huns, go home you huns, go home!' to the tune of 'Auld Lang Syne'. For most of my life, 'hun' wasn't sectarian, it was just a slang word for our biggest rivals. Even to this day no one can say for sure where it came from. But at some point in the last few years it became problematic and fans and even journalists started getting censured for using it.

A couple of years ago, Arsenal's Hector Bellerín was

having a bit of a bad patch after announcing he'd become a vegan, so I said he should get a steak down his neck. Hector had a pop at me on Twitter and a lot of listeners felt the need to complain about me via phone, email and social media. (We actually had a vegan chef on the show once, one of the top guys with a restaurant in Covent Garden. He cooked the food in front of me and it was garbage. I wouldn't have fed it to my dog if it was the last food on earth. But, you know, each to their own.)

Some of the nastier stuff used to get to me, but I'm past that. Now, it's all just banter to me. I'm certainly not one of those people who spends all day scouring social media for abuse so I can have a go back. And I've got no interest in spouting my opinions on social media. I look at someone like Gary Lineker and think, 'Why does he have to tweet everything he thinks?' He's just as entitled to an opinion as anyone else of course, but sometimes I think, 'Jesus, Gary, give it a break. Why invite the hassle?' But some people are just addicted to it.

People also went mad when I said I didn't understand why Andy Murray had blubbed at a press conference after announcing his retirement. I'll admit it, I don't like seeing grown men cry, and I didn't understand what he had to cry about. He'd had a brilliant career, was healthy and had earned a fortune (and I suspected he wasn't going to retire anyway, which he didn't). People have to understand that I don't say things for the sake of an argument or to wind people up, like some radio presenters; that was just my opinion. Ally McCoist and Jim White, who were on the show with me, had a different opinion. McCoist called me 'cold-hearted' and Jim said I was talking 'utter tripe'. That's fine, because that's what the show is all about. Believe me, we didn't fall out about it. But a lot of people, especially young people, are becoming less and less tolerant of people with different opinions from their own.

I did briefly fall out with one of our female newsreaders, Sandy Warr. That all started when I made a joke about Sandy being Jeremy Corbyn's niece, because I didn't think she was being impartial. She took it the wrong way, we had a row on air, and she walked out. I wasn't being nasty or even serious, because I'm not that political anyway. As far as I was concerned I was just saying something I might say to a mate down the pub. But people complained, accusing me of sexism and bullying behaviour. I spoke to Sandy after the show and she was fine. Ofcom, the regulatory body that deals with media complaints, concluded that she'd 'given as good as she got' and that I'd done nothing wrong.

To be honest, I thought the whole episode was a bit patronizing towards Sandy. Did they think she couldn't look after herself because she was a woman? It didn't make any sense to me, because I'd had quite a few on-air ding-dongs with male co-presenters down the years. I'll try to be nice and polite but if someone has a pop at me, I'll give it to them back. I'll have an argument with anyone, whoever it is, don't worry about that. If Jim White tries to be a bit clever, I'll try to cut him down to size. I once told Ian Abrahams to piss off live on air, before telling him he looked like a moose. The next time he came on I introduced him with the words, 'It's 6.30, and here with the news headlines is The Moose . . .' The nickname stuck.

I'm also not afraid to have a row with my guests. At the 2008 Cheltenham Festival, we woke up on the Wednesday to gale-force winds. The course had already been hit by a storm on the Monday, which flattened hospitality tents and tore down fencing, and now it was blowing so hard I thought the roof of the hotel was going to come off. We managed to get ourselves to the studio, but as the morning wore on the tented village had to be evacuated and the organizers became worried that people and horses might be injured, or worse.

Edward Gillespie, the boss of the course, came on the show and said they were going to abandon the day's racing, which seems perfectly reasonable in hindsight. But I wouldn't have it and had a blazing row with him on air.

'You can't abandon it,' I told him.

'What do you mean?'

'You just can't.'

'It's health and safety.'

'But there are tens of thousands of people on their way here.'

'But it's dangerous, Alan.'

'But it's only dangerous in the marquees, not for the horses and jockeys on the course. So just close the marquees and let people watch the racing.'

It just so happened that I'd spoken to the weatherman John Kettley, who we'd get on to talk about how the weather might affect various sporting events, and he'd told me that by 12.30 the gale would have become a breeze, the sun would be out and the rest of the day would be absolutely beautiful. But when I asked Edward how he was going to explain this to the punters, he wasn't interested. So that was that, decision made.

Because I wanted to hammer home my point, when Edward left the studio I said on air, 'Anyone who's made their way down here, I'm heading to a village called Broadway straight after the show. It's about twenty minutes from Cheltenham, it might be the loveliest village in England, and you'll find me in a fantastic little boutique hotel called Russell's. It's going to be a beautiful day, so if anyone fancies a drink in the sun, I'm buying.'

After the show I jumped straight in the car and bombed it down to Broadway. When I turned up at Russell's there were about three hundred people outside, and obviously I had to buy them all a drink. Me and my big mouth. And, lo and behold, at about 12.30 the wind dropped and the sun came out. The cagoules and sweaters came off and we were outside Russell's all afternoon and half the night. What a party we had, one of the best I've had at the festival. Not that Jill was particularly happy when she saw my bill.

Sometimes I'll look at the list of guests and think, 'Have I met this person before? Did I get on with them? Hmmm, I think I might have been a bit critical of them on the show . . .' When you present a show for as long as I have you're bound to have the odd guest on that you've been uncomplimentary about or have met before and didn't get on with. But there's not much you can do about that, you just have to be bold and brassy and get on with it. If you start being hesitant or give any hint that you remember criticizing them &r not getting on with them, they'll sense it and have a pop at you. But if they do have a pop at me, that's not a problem, because it makes for good radio.

It's impossible to agree with everyone and the odd spat is part of what makes live radio so thrilling. But more and more people nowadays disagree with that. People think everything should be 'nice', but I'm a great believer in being honest. If someone asks me a question, I'll tell them what I really think. But these days, being honest can be dangerous. For example, if someone asked me if I'd watch ninety minutes of women's football, I'd say no. Good luck to women footballers and anyone who wants to watch them play, but it's just not my cup of tea. What irritates me is that most people I speak to think the same but are too afraid to say it.

I'll probably have people on my case now, telling me to change my ways and be more open-minded, but I don't care what they think. There are sixty-six million people in the UK and not everyone is going to agree with me. And if you don't like what I say, don't listen to me. I know what my show is all about, what brings in the listeners and the money. And as long as I'm doing that, I'll have a job at talkSPORT. There are 1.5 million people who tune into the show every day who don't seem to have a problem, and that's all that counts.

I know that in some respects people must change with the times, because certain things that weren't offensive ten or twenty years ago are now beyond the pale. But what irritates me is that my listeners have always been what I like to call 'bread and butter' people, much like me. They get up early, listen to my show while they're getting ready for work or driving their van, and all they want is to be cheered up.

Sometimes people in the media say my show is too 'laddish'. But I don't see a problem with being laddish. I don't think I'm being patronizing when I say my listeners aren't complicated people, because I'm not a complicated person either. They tune in to hear me, my co-presenter and our guests talk about sport and the news, have a bit of a laugh and maybe the odd argument. That's it. I believe that if someone is good at their job, it shouldn't matter what sex, colour, nationality, religion, class or age they are. There are people out there who think I'm too old, too manly and too white. But if a radio broadcaster is bringing in listeners, that really should be all that counts.

Like me, my listeners are the sort of people who might have one too many in the pub, turn up for work late the following day and get a bollocking from their boss. They like the fact that I don't pretend to be an angel or broadcasting professional of the year. But hopefully for the four hours I'm on air, I keep them entertained. And that's all I'm worried about.

9

Football Today

While it's true that horseracing replaced football as my first love many years ago, in large part because football has changed so much, there are some things about the modern game that are better than in my day.

Yes, modern football is as soft as it's ever been. In my day, players squared up to each other every game and challenges were wild. If you miscontrolled the ball, someone might come flying in and chop you down from the chest. Usually Souness. And because there weren't always cameras at games – and when there were, there were probably only three at most – a lot of dodgy stuff went on off the ball, like studs down the Achilles and sneaky elbows. Meanwhile, the players' tunnel was sometimes a free-for-all. Stuff that didn't even merit a talking-to from the referee would receive red cards by today's standards. But that's no bad thing. Call me an old softy, but as a player who relied on his skill, I would have loved that level of protection.

Modern stadiums make old grounds look like rubbish dumps. No wonder fans behaved so badly when I was playing, because they were treated like animals. I was at the Ibrox disaster in 1971, when sixty-six Rangers supporters died and more than two hundred people were injured in a crush. I didn't even know it had happened until I got home. But the appalling hooliganism that blighted football during the 1970s and 1980s can't all be blamed on the conditions. During my career I was horrified by some of the abuse dished out to black players. I used to get abused too, for being a Scot. When I got the ball, I'd hear people shouting, 'You Jock wanker! You sweaty bastard!' Anyone who wasn't English got similar treatment. And while it still goes on, and should be punished severely, it's nothing like as bad as it used to be.

Of course, I don't want to see any trouble or disasters now, and I know we're all supposed to believe that a fan's experience is better since stadiums became all-seater in the Premier League era, but something has been lost. I certainly wouldn't swap watching football now with watching football when I was a kid, because I had some of the most exciting days of my life watching Celtic, especially away from home. It was edgy and it was sometimes downright dangerous, but it was also thrilling. And let's be honest, while racist chanting has almost been eradicated, many modern fans are simply abusive about different things. And some of that abuse is every bit as vile as racism.

Former Manchester United and Scotland captain Darren Fletcher has spoken about his experience of opposition fans singing about his health issues (he had ulcerative colitis). Players who have lost children have also been targeted. Then there are the songs teams sing about the Hillsborough and Munich disasters, and the hissing at Spurs fans, which is a 'joke' about the Nazi gas chambers. I cannot get my head around how people can be so hateful. Some people blame alcohol, but I think these people must be sick in the head.

I should add that some of the football in today's Premier League is superb. Jürgen Klopp's Liverpool are a truly great side, with maybe the best forward line ever seen in English football. As a striker, I would have loved to play under Klopp, because the way his team attacks is breathtaking and he's so brimming with enthusiasm that I'd be desperate to do well for him. I played against the great Liverpool sides of the 1980s, with Ian Rush and Kenny Dalglish up front, but Mo Salah, Sadio Mané and Roberto Firmino are also special players. Klopp has also got a brilliant goalkeeper in Alisson, one of the great central defenders in Virgil van Dijk – who is so good that he makes everyone around him look 30 per cent better – and a couple of excellent British full-backs in Trent Alexander-Arnold and Andy Robertson. I don't think you can say Klopp's Liverpool are better than the Liverpool teams of the late 1970s and 1980s quite yet, but if they can keep on winning things for three or four more years, they will be remembered as such.

I saw a quote from Gary Lineker saying that the best modern teams would smash his 1990 England team five- or six-nil. I know what he's getting at, because modern teams are fitter than we were, eat better food and employ more sophisticated training methods. When I was at Ipswich, Bobby Robson was ahead of his time and always telling us to look after ourselves, but there was only so much control a manager could have over his players back then. If we wanted to eat a fry-up after training, we'd eat one. If we wanted to go out on a Thursday night, we'd go out. We might only have four or five halves of lager, but nowadays players would think that was madness – and if they were spotted out on the town two days before a game, they'd get sacked. I wish I'd listened to Bobby a bit more, but that's just how it was in those days.

One of the reasons the drinking wasn't too heavy at Ipswich was because it would sometimes take us six or seven hours to get to and from away games (we didn't have the budget for overnight stays in hotels). Some mornings it would take us about an hour and a half just to reach the M1 or M6. And by the time we got back to Suffolk, all the pubs would be closing up. We'd play a lot of cards on those journeys, and sometimes I'd lose my bonus almost before we'd got out of the car park. Supper would often be fish and chips (the pre-match meal having been boiled chicken or scrambled eggs on toast) and Paul Cooper would sometimes provide a box of bevvies, because his dad was a local publican.

But we didn't drink a huge amount on the bus, because the boss was down the front. Our sponsors Pioneer built us a special bus with a partition, because Bobby and the directors, who were all ancient, hated our music so much. Terry Butcher and Paul Mariner were into some seriously heavy stuff (Mariner was mates with Ian Gillan, the lead singer of Deep Purple), and whenever Bobby pulled the partition aside he'd get blown back towards the driver, as if he'd been hit by a water cannon. I was more into Neil Young, so while Butch and Mariner were head-banging down the back, I'd have my headphones on and be listening to a bit of *Harvest Moon*. What we all agreed on was Roxy Music. Usually when we were getting off the bus before a game, 'Oh Yeah (On The Radio)' would be on the stereo.

Manchester United were famous for their drinking school in the 1980s, but it was no heavier than Liverpool's. That great Liverpool side was full of boozers, as was Brian Clough's Nottingham Forest. The success of those teams certainly had nothing to do with drinking less than other teams. At Tottenham, the bus had two waiters and a fridge full of beer and wine. Whether we drank it all or not, we always made sure we cleaned the fridge out before we got back to the training ground in Cheshunt, otherwise Keith Burkinshaw would cut down on the order. As the players were getting off the bus, you'd be able to hear bottles clinking in their bags.

We'd come off the training ground and have a drink, and we'd all meet up for a drink after a game, at least if we won. We never went to the West End or to private clubs, and if anyone had spent £1,000 on a giant bottle of vodka, Tony Galvin would have reported him to the KGB. Instead, we drank in the Bulls Head in Turnford, just off the A10. The landlord would get his guitar out and we might have a lock-in on a Saturday night. Or we'd go to the Coolbury Club around the corner from White Hart Lane. The landlord was a little Irish guy called Vinnie and we'd drink and banter with the fans.

Bobby Robson was big on basic fitness and obsessive about teeth. He was always telling us to keep our mouths clean and have regular check-ups at the dentist. He used to say, 'If your teeth are healthy, the rest of your body is healthy.' And if a player had a bad tooth he'd give them a bollocking and send them off to the dentist. He also once brought in two psychiatrists to talk to the guys about mental attitude, but that was totally unheard of and very odd. I remember us all taking the piss out of him. But today, psychology and sports science are par for the course.

But who would win between a great old team and a great modern team would all depend on what rules the game was played under. Modern players train and play matches on bowling greens, so I'm not sure how they'd cope on some of the pitches I had to play on – bogs some weeks, sand the next. And players like Bryan Robson and Graeme Souness would smash players like Salah and Manchester City's David Silva and not allow them to play. In those days, that was a legitimate tactic. I'd spend the first ten minutes of almost every game trying to avoid getting injured by a wild tackle. And there's no way a manager like Bobby Robson, Liverpool's Bob Paisley or Nottingham Forest's Brian Clough would allow their team to be thrashed.

Cloughie's teams weren't the most mobile, but every player knew exactly what his job was. Players like Kenny Burns and Larry Lloyd weren't Rolls-Royces, but they were incredible competitors. Kenny was a psycho; he'd kick his granny. And he'd play anywhere Cloughie wanted him to, no argument.

Someone recently sent me a couple of montages of George Best and Jimmy Johnstone, and you can't tell me they wouldn't have been great in today's game. They could do incredible things with a ball and I'd argue that they'd be even better now than they were in their day, because opposition players wouldn't be able to kick them. People go on about how great Lionel Messi and Ronaldo are – rightly so, because they are magnificent footballers – but imagine how good Maradona would be now. He spent most of his career being assaulted by opposition players. Johnny Wark tells me that when he played for Scotland against Argentina at Hampden Park in 1979, when Maradona was still only eighteen, no one could get near him. Every time a Scotland player tried to get the ball off him, they'd just bounce off. So they made the decision to start wellying him instead (Maradona still managed to score his first international goal that day, in a 3-1 Argentina win). But teams can't do that any more, which is why the likes of Johnstone, Best and Maradona would be untouchable today.

The only game that the video assistant referee would have made better was the 1966 World Cup final, because it would have meant Geoff Hurst's second goal being ruled out and maybe England going on to lose to West Germany. (I'm only joking – sort of.) If I was in charge, I'd do away with VAR tomorrow. In fact, I'd call for that room in Stockley Park, where the decisions are made, to be blown up.

Before VAR, I'd slag referees off a lot on my show. I wouldn't be nasty about it, I'd just ask the question, 'How has he not seen that? What was he thinking?' But human error has got to be better than VAR. In fact, I miss human error – it made things interesting. And I'm speaking as someone who is well aware of the pain caused by a controversial offside decision. When I first arrived at Ipswich in 1975 people were still fuming about the officiating in that year's FA Cup semi-final replay against West Ham. Referee Clive Thomas chalked off two goals, including one by Bryan Hamilton, despite the fact that the linesman hadn't raised his flag. West Ham ended up winning 2-1, Bobby Robson called for an inquiry (to no avail), and Ipswich fans of a certain vintage are still grumbling about that decision today. But as annoying as that situation was, at least the decision was made by an official on the field and not a computer in an office on a faceless industrial park somewhere in west London.

I've got no problem with goal-line technology because it's decisive and does the job quickly. But some of the VAR offsides are just ridiculous. Suddenly, goals are being disallowed because a player's elbow or big toe was over the line. How is that giving him an advantage? It's an absolute disgrace, a bad joke. I honestly can't believe it's come to this. And why the referees won't just trot over and look at the monitors on the touchline is beyond me. The people in Stockley Park should say to the ref, 'Go and have a look yourself. We think it might be offside, but make your own mind up. It's your decision.'

VAR is sucking the joy from the game. As a former striker, I know that scoring a goal is the greatest thrill a player can have. But players can't even celebrate any more. The first thing they do is look at the referee or linesman, because they're worried that someone a couple of hundred miles away will have spotted an infringement that took place a couple of plays before the goal.

They're also killing the spontaneous joy of the fans, who are now more reluctant to celebrate a goal in case it gets chalked off. One of the great delights of football is seeing the fans jumping about, cheering and hugging their mates when the ball hits the net. Now they might stand around like lemons for two or three minutes, staring at a screen and not even knowing what the officials in Stockley Park are looking at. I've also noticed that often when VAR disallows a goal, sometimes wrongly, the wind gets knocked out of the attacking team and the defending team goes straight up the other end and scores.

I couldn't agree more with Arsène Wenger, who suggested that if the authorities are going to stick with VAR, they need to change the offside rule. Everyone who's played under Wenger says what a great man he is. People talk about him as if he's some kind of messiah who changed English football when he took over at Arsenal in 1996, so the people in charge should listen to what he has to say. Instead, they're all still huffing and puffing and saying we can't be changing the rules. But they have to change something, because VAR is making the game a farce.

Wenger's proposal was that a player should be onside if any part of his body *that can score a goal* is behind or level with the relevant defender. I'd go further than that and say a player is only offside if there is daylight between him and the defender. If that's the case, there can be no arguments. And the only pass that should be scrutinized is the final pass. When they start winding the tape back and looking for offsides that didn't lead directly to the goal, it baffles people.

Then there are the blatant penalties that are missed. They'll look at it seven or eight times from a variety of angles and still not give it. Who are these people making these decisions? They can't have played the game to any decent level, because if they had, there's no way they would miss the things they do. I've said before that if they are going to persevere with VAR, they should employ ex-refs, ex-players and ex-managers to make the decisions. Stick a combination of three of them in the Stockley Park box and if two of them think it's offside or a penalty, then give offside or a penalty.

Does anyone actually know what the handball rule is nowadays? Is it handball if it hits the shoulder or the collarbone? What about if the ball is smashed at you from point-blank range, or if you're trying to get your arms out of the way? It's like they're making it up as they go along. Sometimes I'll be watching a game at home and get so annoyed I'll have to leave the room. Most of the people I speak to in the pubs think the same. Every time I go out, someone will collar me and say, 'Did you see that VAR decision the other day?'

The biggest irony is, VAR was supposed to rid the game of controversy, but you watch *Match of the Day* and that's all they talk about. I don't even watch the whole of *Match of the Day* now; I spend most of the time fast-forwarding, because all the VAR decisions and discussions about them pain me so much. I'd scrap VAR and introduce four linesmen, although I hear on the grapevine that some bright spark wants to introduce robot referees at the 2022 World Cup in Qatar. Sounds mad, but it can't be much worse than VAR.

I've spoken to some of the current managers about VAR and they won't give me their honest opinion, because they think I might talk about it on the radio or in one of my columns. Everyone in modern football is so guarded about everything, like those players who cover their mouths when they're passing messages on the pitch. What a load of nonsense. In fact, I'm going to make an admission that might surprise you: I don't love football any more, not like I used to. It's given me a great living and I'm honoured to have played for the clubs I played for, as well as my country. I've also met some great people through the game. But do I enjoy the way football is now? Not really.

People often ask me if I'd rather play now than when I did, and the answer is always, 'Absolutely no chance.' I wouldn't fit in the modern game. I know people call me a dinosaur, but they can call me what they like. If I am a dinosaur, I'm a happy one. As far as I'm concerned, I played in the golden age, when players had a dream job and were also able to have fun off the pitch. Some people assume that because modern players have far more money than players from previous eras, they must have a better life. But how many cars does a man really need? And does having lots of cars really make a man happy? Happier than having a catch-up with some old mates?

Don't get me wrong, I've earned a few quid as a broadcaster and I like having nice things. I don't give two hoots about cars, but I've got a nice house in the countryside with a big garden and an apartment in London. But there's more to life than cars and houses. I suppose it just comes down to a different attitude to life.

The landscape has completely changed. When I was playing in the First Division I lived a very normal life, not much different from the man on the street. When I was a kid at Ipswich and living in digs I couldn't wait to get out of the place and go for a couple of pints in my local on a Thursday night. Even when I was at Manchester United, my favourite pub was the Park Hotel in Altrincham, which was run by former Celtic and United star Paddy Crerand. A big night out for me was six pints of Guinness in Paddy's. But do players spend any time with fans today? Or even with each other? I don't think so. They would argue they can't go out, because they've got to behave themselves and they'd be hassled by fans. They've also got camera phones to think of. But you can't tell me that modern players are more popular than George Best was.

Whatever their reasons, that social side of the game seems to have gone. After a game, players lock themselves away in their gated mansions. Maybe they're happy sitting at home playing computer games, watching films in their basement cinema or going to exotic islands with their families. If they are, good luck to them. And when they leave a club, they never speak to their old team-mates again. Maybe that's because they were never really pals in the first place. They never had a beer together, and that banter we had in the dressing room – playing tricks on people, winding people up – didn't exist either.

I still have reunions with my old Ipswich and Tottenham team-mates. Every Christmas, the Spurs lads meet up at Taberna Etrusca on Bow Lane in London and there will be twenty-five of us at least. We'll all meet up at the Sir Bobby Robson Celebrity Golf Classic and raise loads of dough for his charity. Or we'll go to the Algarve for a long weekend, play golf on the Saturday, have dinner on the Saturday night, and spend the whole of Sunday in Julia's beach bar in Almancil. We'll all get up on the mic. Ray Clemence will sing 'You'll Never Walk Alone' and Ossie Ardiles will sing some Sinatra.

I love the banter, like I always did when I was playing. Ossie's wife dresses him, and one year he turned up wearing orange from top to bottom – orange panama hat, orange shirt, orange shorts, orange socks. Because most of the guys flew out with easyJet, the joke was that he looked like one of their cabin crew. Poor old Ossie got slaughtered. Every time he got up, someone would say to him, 'Excuse me, madam, could I have a toastie and some Pringles?' It took him a while to understand, but in the end he was saying, 'I kill my wife, I kill my wife . . .'

While I don't begrudge modern players the money they earn – if the demand is there and someone thinks that's what you're worth, good luck to you – it must have a corrupting influence on youngsters. It can't be right that a kid can be earning fifty grand a week when he hasn't even played a handful of first-team games. Not every kid in that scenario loses focus, but a lot do. If I had earned that kind of money as a teenager, it would have destroyed me. When you're in your early twenties and you're living in a mansion with five supercars in the garage, where's the incentive? The most I earned as a player was £1,500 a week at Manchester United, and that was big money. Our draw and win bonuses meant everything: we relied on them to buy things we otherwise wouldn't have been able to afford. Now, a lot of young players don't care whether they win, lose or draw, because it makes no difference to them financially.

The gap between players and the people who pay a lot of money to watch them makes me feel uncomfortable. I feel for the average punter, because following their team must be a real struggle, especially if they're in the Premier League. Because people love their clubs so much, they will find the money. It doesn't matter where their team is playing in the world, some fans have to be there, even if it bankrupts them. If they can't go to the games, they'll stump up for a TV subscription. And it might not be one subscription, it might be two or three, because nowadays you'll find football on lots of different channels.

If a guy is earning thirty grand a year, how can he take his kids to watch their team play every week? If it's a London team, he's got to pay for the tickets, the travel, food and drink, maybe a programme and a scarf, and it's going to cost hundreds of pounds a pop. Imagine being a dad whose kid is driving you mad to take you to the football and you have to tell him you can't afford it? Or you've got a couple of kids and you can only take one? It would break your heart. And if you can scrape the money together, you might get to watch players on a couple of hundred grand a week, who could retire tomorrow and live in luxury for the rest of their lives, some of whom don't really want to be there and would leave tomorrow if someone offered them more money.

The biggest problem English football has – and it's not just English football – is that there is too much money at the top and not enough of it trickling down. The clubs at the top say, 'It's a business, we've invested in our stadium and our players, and the television companies are only really interested in us. Why should we keep bailing out clubs in the lower leagues who don't run their businesses as well as us?' I think most of them would like the Premier League ring-fenced, so that there is no relegation or promotion. As it is, a handful of big clubs are getting richer and richer and nobody else can compete with them.

I still follow what's going on at Ipswich, and to see them struggling down in League One – they finished the 2019/20 campaign in eleventh place, sandwiched between Gillingham and Burton Albion – breaks my heart. It's difficult to see how they can ever bridge the gap, because getting promoted to the Premier League requires lots of money they haven't got. On top of that, because the big clubs hoard most of the young talent, there are fewer and fewer little gems and late developers in the lower leagues – players like Stan Collymore, who started out at Southend and ended up at Liverpool, and Jamie Vardy, who went from Fleetwood to Leicester before firing them to an unlikely Premier League title in 2015/16.

I think the coronavirus lockdown might lead to sweeping changes in football. The pandemic highlighted exactly how precarious a lot of smaller clubs' finances are. Some of them were clinging on for dear life. As I write, Wigan Athletic, winners of the FA Cup in 2013, have just gone into administration. The Football League has proposed a salary cap for Leagues One and Two, and if that means clubs are able to stay in business then it should be implemented. We've seen too many examples of foreign owners racking up huge wage bills and almost killing clubs with long, proud traditions. And the fans have to accept some of the blame, because they demand the owners spend money. Maybe a salary cap would see the return of a bit more realism in the lower leagues. But you'll never get the big teams to agree to a salary cap, even though it would help make things more competitive and stop clubs from spending beyond their means. They would view it as stifling ambition, while the best players would simply move abroad.

Don't get me wrong, those in charge of the Premier League have done a brilliant job, because it's a huge global brand and awash with money. But it's almost been too successful, because the gap between the established Premier League clubs and everyone else has made the whole league structure more and more unequal and unfair. I know loads of West Ham fans and they're the most disgruntled I've ever met. They're constantly telling me how angry and upset they are and that they want to chuck David Sullivan, David Gold and Karren Brady into the River Lea. But what do West Ham fans want? They simply don't have the money to compete with the top five or six teams. Look at Everton; they've spent fortunes and are still struggling to make an impression. And if they can't break into the top five or six, what chance have West Ham got?

The mad part is, the Premier League is more competitive than most of the big leagues in Europe. In Italy, Juventus have won the last nine league titles in a row; in Germany, Bayern Munich have won eight titles in a row; in France, Paris Saint-Germain have won seven of the last eight titles; in Spain, either Barcelona or Real Madrid have won fifteen of the last sixteen titles; in Holland, Ajax and PSV Eindhoven have won sixteen titles between them since the beginning of the twenty-first century; in Portugal, either Benfica or Porto have won the last seventeen titles; and in Scotland, Celtic have won nine titles in a row and no other team apart from the Hoops and Rangers has won a title since 1985.

Let's face it, having the same teams win their leagues all the time is unhealthy and pretty boring. When sport is at its best, it's unpredictable. But some seasons I find myself almost ignoring what's happening at the top of the Scottish Premiership table, because I know who's going to win it; I spend the last few months more intrigued by what's happening at the bottom and who might be relegated. That can't be good. I'll get stick for saying this, but without a strong Rangers side, Scottish football will dwindle and die. Of course I want Celtic to win trophies, but I don't want Celtic to win almost every game.

I was happy to see some of the Old Firm needle back during the 2019/20 season. After Rangers' win at Celtic

Park, people were going on about how badly everyone had carried on. But that was a sign that the rivalry is competitive again, which can only be a good thing. Not even the most ardent Celtic fans can want it to be a one-horse race every season. Surely? Then again, Old Firm thuggery ain't like it used to be. In the aforementioned game, Celtic's Ryan Christie grabbed Rangers' Alfredo Morelos by his crown jewels and was given a two-game ban. The SFA called it 'brutality'. Brutality? When I watched Old Firm games as a kid, players would be snarling and elbowing and kicking each other in the air for ninety minutes. For how Rangers' John Greig dealt with Jimmy Johnstone, he could have been done for GBH on at least ten occasions. It was that gamesman-ship and skulduggery that really got the crowd going.

Ally McCoist and I are always talking about what's gone wrong with Scottish football. In the 1980s, the English First Division was packed with Scottish talent. Liverpool had Kenny Dalglish, Graeme Souness, Alan Hansen and Steve Nicol; Manchester United had Arthur Albiston, Joe Jordan, Gordon McQueen and Gordon Strachan; Nottingham Forest had Kenny Burns and John Robertson; at Ipswich there was me, George Bur-ley and Johnny Wark, before he moved to Liverpool. Almost every team had at least one Scottish player. Now there are hardly any Scottish stars in the Premier League, which is frightening. There's Andy Robertson at Liver-pool, Kieran Tierney at Arsenal, Billy Gilmour at Chelsea and Scott McTominay at Manchester United, although even he was born and raised in England. But there's not much else. And when young talent does turn up, they're not thrown into international football early enough. Gilmour should have been in Scotland's senior squad when he was eighteen, when he was already holding his own in the Premier League. The lad was even man of the match against Liverpool. It's irrelevant that he's not playing a lot for Chelsea, because at Stamford Bridge he's battling for a starting spot with world-class players like the Italy international Jorginho. He's a fine player and seems grounded and assured. I hope he becomes a Scotland regular soon.

I can't tell you exactly why the talent in Scotland has dried up, but clearly the schools and the Scottish FA haven't been doing their jobs properly for a long time, because the national team hasn't qualified for a major tournament in the twenty-first century. And to be more competitive, and to produce better players, the Scottish Premiership has got to strike a better television deal. The money Scottish teams get from broadcasting rights is pathetic compared to teams in the English Premier League, and the relative lack of money and competition means few top players from other countries want to play there. Unless we can develop talented kids and keep them in Scotland for a few years before they join English clubs, we're unlikely to get much more money out of the broadcasters, because the product won't be worth watching.

Of course, another way to improve Scottish football would be for Celtic and Rangers to join the English Premier League. But I can't see that happening any time soon, because while it would benefit the Old Firm,

plenty of English clubs would view them as two potentially mighty competitors. If it did happen, neither side
would be in with a chance of winning the title the first
few years after joining. But once that TV money started
kicking in and they were able to compete for the biggest
players in the transfer market, things would get interesting. They're massive football clubs with huge followings.
And who wouldn't want to play at a rocking Celtic Park
or Ibrox every week, especially if Liverpool or Manchester United were the visitors?

The way things are going, European super league seems
inevitable. I think the TV companies will end up demanding it, and because the world is getting smaller and
smaller it will make perfect sense to many people. You'll
still have the traditionalists, especially supporters of
teams outside the Premier League, who will be dead set
against it. But I think it will reach a point where even
the fans of Liverpool, both the Manchester teams, Chelsea, Arsenal and Tottenham will see an elite European
league as making more sense.

Some of Europe's top clubs are already lobbying to
transform the Champions League into a thirty-two-team
league. Their proposal has nothing to do with football,
it's all about money and the biggest teams in Spain, Italy,
France and Germany trying to grab more of it. They've
watched the Premier League become richer and richer
and they see a revamped Champions League as a way of
bridging the gap. Luckily, their proposal is so unwieldy
and daft that people aren't falling for it. At the moment.

But I can see the likes of Real Madrid, Barcelona and Juventus getting their way eventually. And once they do, the revamped European super league will be a closed shop. Instead of teams being able to reach this elite league via promotion, I fear those big teams will say 'Sorry, lads, you're not invited' and pull up the ladder. They don't want to be sharing any cash with the continent's 'minnows'. And that will mean saying goodbye to Celtic and Rangers, Club Brugge and Anderlecht in Belgium, Malmö in Sweden, Panathinaikos in Greece, and the list goes on.

For years people have been saying the Premier League bubble is going to burst but it just gets bigger and bigger. And because more and more people are demanding the Premier League as a product, the Premier League think they should have more and more of the money. I can remember David Sheepshanks, the former chairman of Ipswich who was also involved with the Football League, constantly asking for a few more crumbs from the Premier League table, only to be told the big boys were against it. And things have got worse over the last fifteen years or so.

But you'd be naive to think that the bubble will never burst in England, because we've already seen it happen elsewhere. It wasn't too long ago that Italy's Serie A was the biggest and most exciting league in the world, but attendances dropped off alarmingly as the twenty-first century wore on. I'm not saying English fans should stop going to games, but maybe they should start saying, 'Hold on a minute, maybe it's time for a cap on ticket prices. This is no longer a sport for working-class people.

And I'm getting a bit bored of my team having absolutely no chance of winning anything for decades at a time.'

On top of all that, the owners of some of these clubs are as dodgy as anything. When I was at Ipswich, the owners were a couple of eccentric English aristocrats who owned a brewery. Yes, they were wealthy, but not beyond anyone's wildest dreams. In contrast, nobody seems to know where some of these modern owners are getting their money from and nobody seems to care. Are the rules on ownership as strict as they should be? There's all this money pouring in from places like China and India, from individuals who are richer than most people on the planet put together, yet they've got millions of people in their own country living in poverty. And when I say poverty, I mean poverty like the vast majority of British people couldn't really understand.

Then you've got all the money coming in from the Middle East, including from the Abu Dhabi royal family, who own Manchester City. It's not a secret that the United Arab Emirates has a terrible human rights record – it's been widely reported on – and Newcastle came close to being taken over by Saudi Arabia. Had that happened, Newcastle fans wouldn't have cared where the money was coming from if it enabled them to buy some decent players and win something. Morals just seem to go out of the window when it comes to sport. It doesn't seem to matter how dodgy the owners may be, most fans love their club so much that they will carry on watching regardless.

*

Agents are another big issue in modern football. I've got no problem with many of them, who just want to get the best deal for their players. At the same time there are a lot of agents who don't have their clients' best interests at heart. A good agent will say to a player, 'There are a couple of clubs interested in you, but you need to consider whether it's the right time to move. You can earn more money elsewhere, but you won't be guaranteed a place in the team. If you stay here, you'll be playing every week and getting better and better. You'll make a name for yourself, become a fans' hero and then you'll get the big move in a couple of seasons.' Instead, these agents are saying to players, 'Listen, son, I've got two clubs showing a lot of interest in you, and they're offering a lot more than you're currently getting. Don't worry about your contract, that's not worth the paper it's written on. You'll get a big signing-on fee, you'll be able to get a new house, that Bentley you wanted, and you can look after your mum and dad . . .' I consider this a form of brainwashing, and it's horrible to witness.

Most players aren't mature enough to turn round and say, 'No thanks. I think I should abide by my contract. This club has treated me well, we're winning matches, and I'm learning as a footballer. Come back to me in eighteen months and we'll talk.' Instead, they'll be thinking, 'God, if I could be earning twice as much elsewhere, my club obviously don't rate me . . .' Immediately, that kid is unsettled, his focus has gone, and maybe he thinks he's going to be the next world superstar. Once a player starts thinking like that, he stops concentrating on the here and now and becomes obsessed with what might be. He doesn't care as much about playing for his current club and stops trying to improve, because he doesn't think he's going to be there for much longer.

When a player gets his 'dream' move, he often ends up sitting in the dugout for a couple of seasons, when he could have been the main man at his previous club. How many times have we seen it happen? Then again, I'm not convinced some of these players are even that bothered. I couldn't stand being a substitute; I was always dying to get on. But as long as some of these modern players are getting a big cheque at the end of the month, they're happy warming the bench.

I don't think that's the case with Manchester City's Phil Foden, because he's been at the club since he was a little kid. But the time has come for him to make a decision. Is he happy to be a bit-part player? Or does he want to be playing football every week, even if that means moving to a smaller club? I know he's still only twenty, but you've got to make the most of every second when you're a professional sportsperson. He might get a bad injury, as happened to me. And before he knows it he'll be in his late twenties. It's not an easy decision, but I hope he doesn't look back and think he wasted some of his best years.

In a sane world – which football isn't – something would be done to cap how much money academy players can earn. A couple of years ago I wrote a *Sunday Post* column about a lad called George Green, who received a £45,000 signing-on fee from Everton and was immediately dubbed 'the new Wayne Rooney'. Just to remind you, when I joined Ipswich I was on £14 a week. My first professional contract was £55 a week, and I had to pay for my digs out of that.

In Everton's youth teams, George played alongside Ross Barkley and John Stones. By the age of nineteen he was earning £110,000 a year, despite never playing for the first team. And one of the reasons he never played for the first team was because by the age of eighteen he was already spending thousands of pounds a week on drink and drugs. Last I heard, he had cleaned up his act but was out on loan at Gainsborough Trinity.

George was a young kid who couldn't handle that much wealth and didn't have people around him giving him sensible advice. But nothing will be done to prevent more George Greens from happening, because even if the authorities do cap earnings for youth team players, clubs will think of other clever ways to convince talented young players to join them.

As I said, many agents don't care about their clients' careers or a football club's history or reputation, all they care about is selling their client for as much money as possible. Because the more money an agent can prise out of a club, the more money they make personally. These agents are taking millions of pounds out of football (FIFA stated that agents earned £500 million in 2019 alone) and putting nothing back in. FIFA is right to introduce a cap on the amount agents can make from transfers, because they're holding clubs to ransom. And I'm not surprised that some of these 'super' agents are planning to sue, because someone like Paul Pogba's representative Carmine Raiola stands to earn a fortune when his client is finally offloaded by Manchester United.

Raiola is very good at his job, which is moving players around to make millions out of them, but he's been taking the piss out of United. Alex Ferguson sussed Raiola a long time ago, which is why he called him a 'shitbag'. If Fergie was still in charge of United he would have told Raiola and Pogba to get stuffed a long time ago. Then again, I'm not sure Fergie would have got away with it now, because players have so much more power and are softer than they used to be. Nowadays, Fergie would be accused of bullying. And imagine Paul Pogba playing for Brian Clough. Cloughie was a genius, but some of his methods were extreme. Those two would have fallen out after a few minutes. I've always said that if I was Ole Gunnar Solskjaer, I'd have driven Pogba to the airport myself. Cloughie would have tied him to his roof rack.

I know Pogba is a World Cup winner and a top player when he's on his game (and people tell me he's a nice lad away from football), but I don't see the greatness and I can't stand his attitude. It's not entirely his fault, because clubs and sponsors have lavished massive amounts of money upon him, which is always going to give a player an inflated sense of his own worth. But does he want to play for United or doesn't he? If he doesn't, then he should piss off. It's not like United would miss him that much, and they would still get a lot of money for him. I'm amazed the United fans have put up with him for so long. Even George Best didn't get away with it. In the end, George had to sling his hook, and he was a far better player than Pogba, don't you worry about that.

As for stats, I absolutely hate them. Opta is the current official provider of analysis to the Premier League, and I'd go so far as to say that most of their statistics are a load of bollocks, even though the numbers themselves might be correct. Goals, fine. Shots on target, fine. Assists, fine. But passes? So what if someone passed the ball fifty times? It's meaningless unless we know what those passes led to. Then you get stats on how often a player gives the ball away. Well, if that player is just passing the ball sideways to people standing a few yards away, the fact that he never gives the ball away is irrelevant. Someone might attempt ten through balls in a game and only pull two of them off, but those two successes might lead to two goals. Stuff the eight unsuccessful through balls, they don't matter; at least that player was trying to create something. I know managers use stats, but they'll know full well that they can be misleading. That's why most sensible managers will want to see someone play a few times before signing them, because it's their eyes that will tell them whether a player is any good or not, not stats on a screen.

The reason stats have become so popular with journalists is because too many of them have never played football to any decent level and don't know enough about what they're watching. They use stats as a crutch and fill their reports with numbers because they're unable to analyse the action using words. I'll hear them say, 'So-and-so didn't give the ball away once but he only touched the ball thirty times,' and I'll be thinking, 'But did he have a good game?' Who gives a shit how many times he touched the ball; did he do anything with it when he had it? Stats are just part of the story, not the whole story.

Too many football journalists nowadays think we care about their opinion, when all I want from them is an accurate report of the game. Who played well? Did so-and-so create much? Did so-and-so cause the other team much trouble? Did so-and-so spend enough time in the box? That's the kind of stuff I want to know. But some modern football journalists have become starstruck and got really carried away. They're doing radio phone-ins, giving their expert opinions on TV, doing analytical podcasts. Some of them should just stick to what they're good at, which is writing a nice match report.

You only have to look at the player ratings they have in newspapers to see how much some football journalists know about the game. I read them sometimes and think, 'Was this person actually at the game? He must have been watching it in the pub with his mates and spent most of his time on the fruit machine.' Even some of the commentators have lost the plot. A commentator is there to tell people what's happening – the raw, basic facts – not why it's happening. That's what the co-commentators and pundits are for, because they've been there and done it. So many people nowadays, in all walks of life, think they know about stuff they've never experienced.

10

Not Slowing Down

People are always asking me when I'm going to slow down. But why would I want to slow down when there is still so much fun to be had? The weird part is, I'm the complete opposite to my parents. My dad used to worry about everything, so he never went out or spent any money. And not only did he not drink, he wouldn't let my mum have many either. She'd have the odd glass of wine, but after a couple she'd lose the power of speech. It takes a few more than that to make me start talking gibberish, although some people might disagree.

When I tell people I've been a good boy and not drunk for four or five days, they'll look at me like I've gone mad. People assume I've got a drink problem, but that's simply not the case. Sometimes I just won't feel like going to the pub and will stay at home with the family instead. That keeps me sane. I actually get drunk very rarely, because I like to keep my wits about me. My ability to drink a lot isn't something I'm particularly proud of, but some people can cope, some people can't. I just love being sociable, and our time on earth is not a rehearsal. I think some people are envious that I'm able to drink quite a bit and still do my job.

That said, there's no doubt I've overdone things in the past, which has led to the odd misjudgement. In 2008 I was nicked for drink-driving, which is obviously not something I'll want to tell the grandchildren about. On the Saturday morning I'd done a show on talkSPORT before driving to Ely for a charity fundraiser for a hospital in Cambridge. The plan was to do my bit and stick around for a few glasses of wine, then get a taxi to a hotel the organizers had arranged for me. But when I turned up, a hotel hadn't been booked, and I had to follow a taxi to the middle of a big field where a marquee had been set up. Afterwards, taxis were taking ages to get to the venue and eventually I lost patience and decided to drive home myself.

I was coming up to Bury St Edmunds, tootling along with the window down, minding my own business, when flashing lights appeared from nowhere. I pulled over, got out of the car, and knew right away from the attitude of the policeman that someone from the event had grassed me up. I said to the copper, 'Was there a problem with my driving?' and he replied, 'This is a 70mph zone and you were doing 50mph.' I was actually doing 55mph, because I had the cruise control on. But there was no point in arguing. I swear on my children's lives that I wasn't even close to being drunk, but I'll admit I'd probably had a couple too many.

At Bury St Edmunds police station I had seven goes on the big breathalyser machine before it gave a reading. They said I wasn't blowing hard enough, to which I replied, 'Mate, with the greatest respect, I talk for a living. If I haven't got enough puff to make this machine work, no one has.' Having ascertained I was over the limit, I thought they'd let me get a cab home. Instead, they decided I deserved a night in the cells. I thought that was totally unnecessary – it's not like I was a terrorist or a paedophile and a threat to the public. The following morning there was a different desk sergeant on duty. He said to me, 'I've just looked over the case. You were polite and didn't swear, so I don't know why you got banged up.' I replied, 'I suggest you ask your mate!'

My court case got cancelled over and over again, until eventually I was found guilty at a magistrates' court, banned for twenty months and fined about a grand. That was expected, although my lawyer said that a judge might have let me off. What wasn't expected was that the video of my police interview and breathalyser test would end up in the hands of the newspapers. People told me I should have sued them, but my wife told me to forget it. She was right, of course. It was a stupid thing to have done and it was time to move on.

As far as I'm concerned, once I've finished the show at ten o'clock I can do what I want for the rest of the day. Because the talkSPORT offices have always been in the heart of London, first on the South Bank and then in the News Building at London Bridge, me and my co-presenters have had some epic days and nights out in the capital. When people ask when I peak during the day, I usually reply, 'About twenty-two minutes after the show is over, when I'm in Goodman's steak house, Old Jewry.'

Another favourite haunt of mine is the Italian restaurant Taberna Etrusca, next to St Mary-le-Bow church (within the sound of whose bells a Cockney must be born) – the place where the Spurs lads meet for their Christmas do. We'll have a bit of lunch, and when everyone else goes back to work the owner, Enzo, brings out a stereo and we all play Name That Tune. In the summer there will be eight or nine of us sat around the table in the courtyard – me and a few other characters from talkSPORT, plus bankers and brokers who have taken the afternoon off work – the wine will be flowing, and we might not get out of there until ten, especially if it's a Friday. Sometimes when we're all having a sing-song, the workers in the offices above will join in.

And who knew that you could find a champagne bar in Waitrose? Not me, until I bought an apartment in Canary Wharf and Jill sent me out shopping one lunchtime. The last words she said before I left were, 'Don't be too long.' Anyway, I was wandering around Waitrose, loading up the trolley, when suddenly I spotted three different bars at the far end. I couldn't believe my eyes; it was like a mirage. It was full of ladies who lunch and bankers, all having a grand old time, so I thought to myself, 'This'll do me, I'll have a quick glass of wine.'

One glass led to another, people started coming up to me and chatting to me about the show, and three hours later I was still in there. Eventually I realized I hadn't got all the shopping I was supposed to and went back out with my trolley, before heading back to the bar for a few more glasses.

I didn't get home until gone eight o'clock, and when I walked through the door, Jill said, 'Where the hell have you been?'

'Shopping.'

'For five hours? You've been in the shop for five hours?'

'Yeah, it's got three bars. It's brilliant.'

Now, I often have business meetings in there. People say to me, 'What restaurant shall we meet in?'

'Waitrose,' I reply.

'You what?'

'You'll see what I mean when you get there.'

People finish work at five to 5.30, pop down for a couple of beers and don't want to go home. And if you fancy a bit of dinner, they've got a steak and oyster bar as well. By eight o'clock the doormen are throwing people out. I take Ray Parlour down there every now and again, because it's easy for him to get the train back to Essex. The problem with Parlour is that he gets pissed very easily. Well, when I say he gets pissed very easily, he always seems to be pissed when I'm OK, which baffles people: 'How come he can't talk and you're fine?' One evening Parlour had a few too many, recorded a video of me doing my shopping – each to their own – and posted it on social media. That was all well and good, but then someone filmed him on the train home, hanging on to a pole while fast asleep. I think the second clip got far more hits.

Whenever I'm out there are always people wanting to have a chat, whether it's about the show, football, horseracing, wine or whatever. Very occasionally someone will have a pop at me, but the vast majority of people are respectful. Sometimes people can go on a bit, especially when they've had a bit too much to drink. But I've learned the art of slipping away politely. Usually I'll say, 'Jesus, is that the time? Sorry, pal, I've really got to go because I'm getting picked up. Thanks for a lovely chat, have a great night, and don't go too mad.' A few minutes later I'll probably be in the bar next door.

If any of my co-presenters are out with me, they always struggle to keep up, whether it's McCoist, Parlour, The Moose or anyone else. Steve Harmison drinks like he bowled: he starts off at a furious pace but is flagging after a few pints. He'll always aim to get the 1.30 train back to Darlington, but that usually gets put back to 3.30, and then 6.30. The next time I see him he'll invariably tell me he can't remember leaving the pub.

After a few beers, my co-presenters often make the mistake of telling me things in confidence, which I then tease them about on the show. At Cheltenham one year, Dominic Cork informed me that his missus had ordered him to stick to drinking halves. I said to him, 'Have you gone mad? You can't be drinking halves in the Guinness tent.' But he was adamant, so the following morning I nicknamed him 'Half Pint Corky' live on air. After the show we headed to the Guinness Village and every few minutes someone would shout, 'All right, Half Pint? You go easy today or your missus will be upset.' Corky gave me a withering look and said, 'Why do I tell you things?' He should have known better.

Because people who host breakfast radio shows are among the few employed people who can sit in a pub all day, I occasionally have a day out with one of my rivals. Chris Evans, who's now on Virgin Radio, has been a mate for years. Recently, he phoned me up and said, 'Right, next Wednesday, Al, are you up for it?' Chris has a reputation as a bit of a hellraiser but has been looking after himself these last few years, running marathons and the like for charity, so I wondered how he was going to cope after two or three glasses.

On meeting at a hotel at London Bridge, Chris started ordering tequilas for him and his team. That wasn't for me, not at that time in the morning. After a couple of hours we headed for the Ned, which is just down the road from Bank and one of my favourite places in London. Once we'd settled into our usual corner, Chris produced a bottle of red from his bag. It was a Petrus Pomerol 2005, which I immediately knew was a lot of money.

I said to him, 'What are we going to do with this?'

'We can drink this in the minivan on the way to the next bar.'

'You're having a laugh! We can't open a bottle of Petrus while we're pub-hopping.'

'Don't worry, I've got loads of them.'

As it turned out, Chris only lasted about another hour. The last I saw of him he was bouncing off walls towards the exit, not to be seen again that day. Meanwhile, I was left carrying this bottle of Petrus Pomerol in a plastic bag. The moral of that story? Don't start drinking tequilas at eleven o'clock in the morning, especially when you don't really drink much any more.

The following day, I called one of Chris's mates to see if he was OK and was told that he wanted to do it all again. I said, 'What do you mean, he wants to do it all again? We were supposed to have a few nice glasses of wine and maybe a bit of lunch and he lasted less than two hours. Tell him to stay off the tequila.' He also insisted I keep the bottle of Petrus, which I'd mentioned on that morning's show.

After the show I headed to Waitrose in Canary Wharf, where I sat next to the special temperature-controlled room where all the really expensive wine is kept. I was nursing a glass of white when this elderly couple walked past and gave me a sideways look, before grabbing the wine expert and disappearing into this special room.

When they re-emerged, I said, 'Did you find anything you liked?'

The lady replied, 'No. We're big listeners of your show and wanted to find the bottle of Petrus that Chris Evans gave you.'

I fished the Petrus out of the plastic bag and said, 'This one?'

'Yes! That's the one. They have it, but it's £3,000 a bottle.'

Before she said that, I was thinking about giving it to them.

When I got home, I showed Jill the bottle of wine, told her how much it cost, and she snatched it out of my hands. I went to fetch a couple of glasses and Jill said, 'We're not drinking that, we're saving it for the kids.'

As it turned out, the kids didn't benefit from it either. When Chris started auctioning off a load of his memorabilia for the NHS charity Scrubs Glorious Scrubs and asking his celebrity mates for donations, I suggested we auction the Petrus plus a slap-up lunch at Langan's Brasserie with me, Chris and Ray Parlour. The winning bid was £23,500! It will be some of the best money they ever spent, because those charity Langan's lunches are legendary. People fall over, don't make it home, end up staying in hotels and waking up the following morning not knowing why they're there or where they've been.

Another charity I like to support is the Celtic FC Foundation, which puts on events all over the UK to raise money for various good causes. A guy from Glasgow called Gavin Kelly got me involved with the Celtic FC Foundation. Gavin grew up down the road from me but went to a posh Catholic school called St Aloysius and ended up being some big-shot financial guy in London. Because Gavin was a massive Celtic fan I'd met him at various events down the years, including a big party at the Victoria and Albert Museum where Bryan Ferry and his band were the cabaret. A few years ago now, Gavin phoned me and said, 'Listen, it's coming up to fifty years since Celtic won the European Cup. Do you fancy putting on a little gig?'

I immediately replied, 'Of course we should.'

The only problem was, Gavin was such a big Celtic fan and so ambitious that he wanted to put on a lunch at the Grosvenor House Hotel on Park Lane, which I never thought they'd go for. Hosting hundreds of rowdy football fans isn't really the Grosvenor's thing. But we had several meetings, managed to put everything together, and it became this enormous event. Some of the Lisbon Lions came down for it, loads of Celtic fans descended on the place, and the poor Grosvenor staff didn't know what had hit them. It was like a battle scene from *Braveheart*, with people wearing Celtic shirts and kilts lying in the car park and kipping in the park over the road.

Eventually I managed to fight my way into the hotel's Great Room and there must have been fifteen hundred people in there. There were banners everywhere, from Celtic supporters clubs the length and breadth of the country, and the place was absolutely jumping. We'd managed to get some of the richest people in Scotland to attend, Formula 1's Eddie Jordan hosted, and my old mates Simple Minds and Susan Boyle provided the entertainment. The wildlife photographer and conservationist David Yarrow, who's from Glasgow, donated a magnificent picture of a lion called Caesar and we raised £2 million on the night. It was a sensational effort from everyone involved.

Every now and again, when I need a break from London, I'll take one of my co-presenters on a foreign adventure. A few years ago Ray Parlour and I were invited to Singapore by this fella we know called Goughie. Goughie played junior football in Scotland, moved to Hong Kong and ended up getting involved in a lighting business. Before we went, I had no idea how big or small this business was – I thought we might turn up and find him rattling around in a ramshackle hardware shop selling light bulbs, like in the famous *Two Ronnies* 'Four Candles' sketch.

The plan was for me to give a talk at Singapore Cricket Club and for Ray to play in a soccer sixes tournament. Ray brought along a mate of his from Essex called Mac, and the three of us met Goughie straight off the plane and went directly to the cricket club. When Goughie started telling me that he also owned property in London, I realized that his business was a little bit more substantial than I'd suspected.

Singapore Cricket Club, situated right in the heart of the city, was every bit as magnificent as I expected. The dinner was packed, my talk went down a storm, and once I was done I was able to put my feet up and relax. Over drinks, Goughie told me that he'd been banned from the cricket club on a few occasions, for what you might call 'boisterous behaviour'. On the day of the Grand National, he and some mates set up a course in the clubhouse consisting of chairs and tables, and when the committee found out they revoked his membership. Three months later Goughie was brought in front of a jury and had to plead to be let back in: 'I'm so sorry. It's not just the drink, it's also the heat. I'm from Scotland, I'm just not used to it . . .' Then there would be another episode and he'd have to go through the process all over again.

The following day we decided to have a few drinks at the famous Raffles Hotel. Ray had to train, which gave him the right hump, so I headed down there with his mate Mac. When we walked into the Long Bar there were monkey nut shells all over the floor, which is apparently a tradition, leading all the way back to the days of Somerset Maugham and Rudyard Kipling. But Mac was more interested in Singapore Slings than monkey nuts. I don't normally drink spirits or cocktails, but I decided to make an exception just this once.

After three or four Singapore Slings, Mac was getting a little bit happy. The barman wouldn't tell me what was in them but suggested we be careful and take it easy. Mac wasn't listening. He carried on chucking them back at a rare old pace, while grumbling that it was like drinking with his nan. A few hours later Ray turned up and they started giving us freebies, with the waiter shaking Singapore Slings at our table. And a few hours after that, Goughie turned up with his business partner Chinese Eddie.

Goughie and Chinese Eddie couldn't understand why the bar was giving us free drinks, so I collared the manager and asked him. The manager replied, 'Sir, you are a legend. Ollie Reed was in here once, drank nineteen Singapore Slings and had to be carried out. But you are still standing.' I asked him how many we'd had, and he replied, 'Thirty-seven between you.' After a blistering start, Mac was now lagging behind me, so I'm pretty sure I outdid Ollie.

The following morning we were playing golf. But

when we picked Mac up from his hotel, he was looking terrible. When I asked if he was OK, he said his heart was going like the clappers. After three holes he jumped in his buggy and headed in the direction of the club-house. The rest of us managed to get nine holes in before a thunderstorm washed us off the course. When Mac walked into the clubhouse a few hours later, he looked like a ghost. It turned out he'd thought he was having a heart attack and got a cab to rush him to hospital. But instead of a heart attack, the sugar in the cocktails had sent his blood pressure through the roof. For the rest of the day I kept saying to him, 'If I'm your nan, what does that make you?'

That day we avoided Singapore Slings and stayed on champagne. After a few drinks, I said to Goughie, 'With all due respect, how have you made so much money sell-ing light bulbs?'

He replied, 'We don't sell light bulbs, you idiot.'

As it turned out, their business had offices in Singa-pore, Hong Kong and Indonesia, and they did lighting for hotels and casinos all over Asia.

Goughie is one of the funniest guys I've met, a classic Jock who doesn't stop drinking until he falls over. I've met Scotsmen like him all over the world, people who have left their homeland, become incredibly successful but never really changed.

I still see my old mate Jim Kerr from Simple Minds and he hasn't changed a bit since our days at Holyrood School either. Him and Charlie Burchill pop into the studio every now and again and they're an absolute joy.

Old childhood friends turn up in the most unlikely places. After the 2004 Cheltenham Festival (when I got sacked), I was sitting outside Russell's restaurant in the village of Broadway when an old friend called Dessie Reilly walked past. I hadn't seen him since the Ibrox disaster in 1971. Another time, I was having lunch at the Savoy and a couple of old schoolmates just wandered in.

One of my dearest old school pals, Arthur Gordon, ended up being a stockbroker in London and had two children by the Marquess of Bath's daughter, but never stopped being a proper Glaswegian. Arthur was a decent footballer, is still a massive Celtic man, and we see each other often, because he works in Canary Wharf. Arthur tells a great story about the time his wee boy went back to school after the summer holidays. The teacher asked the class what they'd been up to and he got the usual replies: one said that he'd been to the pictures with his mum, another said he'd been swimming with his dad. Then Arthur's son said, 'We went to Grandpa's house and fed his monkeys and lions.' When the teacher next saw Arthur, he said to him, 'Wow, your boy has got an incredible imagination. Just fantastic.' Arthur asked him what he meant, the teacher described what his son had told him, and Arthur had to explain that his boy's grandfather owned Longleat Safari Park.

When I'm back in Glasgow, I normally head to a pub on Govanhill, which is between Hampden Park and the Gorbals. That's where I feel most comfortable, because I'll be with old school pals and not get any bother. Ally

McCoist might take us to some dodgier areas, but I'm always a little bit wary. I love Glaswegians and some of them seem to like me. The last time I did a book signing in Glasgow, there were 250 people queuing out of the door. But there's usually the odd nutter hanging around. And because I have strong opinions about football, I irritate people. For example, some Celtic fans hate me for saying Scottish football needs a strong Rangers side. But that's life.

I'm very proud of my Scottish heritage. The Scots have big hearts and are very clever people. Look at all the Scottish scientists and inventors: John Napier, who invented logarithms; James Watt, the Godfather of the Industrial Revolution; Joseph Black, who discovered carbon dioxide; Lord Kelvin, he of the Kelvin temperature scale; Alexander Fleming, who discovered penicillin; Alexander Graham Bell, who built the first telephone; John Logie Baird, one of the inventors of television . . . the list is endless. And we're still producing very talented people today, whether it's in science, the arts, literature, pop music and pretty much everything else. There will be people reading this thinking 'Scotland hasn't produced many great footballers of late', and they would be right. But we produce some great talents in other sports, including Andy Murray in tennis, Chris Hoy in cycling and Katherine Grainger in rowing.

I've now lived in England three times longer than I lived in Scotland, but Scotland will never not be my spiritual home. Whenever someone asks me where I'm from, I always say Glasgow. My wife is English, but my daughters are fifty-fifty, and two of them skied for Scotland as kids. I could never move back there full-time because my eldest daughter Michelle has three girls, but one day I'd like to buy a little place up in the Highlands which we could visit in the winter and get away from it all. Like the Irish, the Scots are great adventurers. They like to roam and see what the rest of the world is like. But they never stop being Scottish or proud of where they came from.

Many people born in England to Scottish parents are as fiercely proud of their heritage as people born north of the border. Rod Stewart springs to mind. After the incident when I almost got into a fight with a load of Rangers fans at Glasgow Airport I decided never to go to another Old Firm game. But then Rod, with whom I'd stayed in touch since the 1982 World Cup, invited me up for a game at Celtic Park in his private jet, which I couldn't really turn down. That happened a couple of times. We'd meet at Stansted Airport, fly up to Glasgow, get picked up on the tarmac, watch the game, and fly straight back home.

Rod listens to my breakfast show from his house in Los Angeles and we text each other all the time. When the Celtic fans turned against him recently, he was heartbroken. They weren't happy when he was awarded a knighthood in 2016 and even angrier when he congratulated Boris Johnson on winning the 2019 election. They unveiled an enormous banner at Celtic Park that said 'Fuck Off Rod'. Charming. I couldn't believe what I was seeing, because they were talking about a man who has Celtic in his blood and adores the club.

These people have it wrong if they think his support of Celtic and Scotland is a gimmick. I once spent a night at his house in Essex and one of the rooms was like a shrine to the Hoops. His Celtic knowledge is encyclopaedic. When he does a concert, the bass drum has the Celtic badge on it. I understand that Celtic is a working-class club and most people in Glasgow aren't big fans of the Tories, but how can open displays of sectarianism be frowned upon when they're happy to abuse people who happen to have different political beliefs? He's also raised millions of pounds for various charities, including for the NHS during the coronavirus pandemic (he even donated a Celtic shirt signed by the Lisbon Lions), so how dare Celtic fans give him stick. I don't get that kind of attitude, it makes no sense to me.

Like my daughters, Rod is a product of a multi-cultural Britain where people have heritage from all over the globe. My granddaughters' other grandfather is Greek, so we're regular visitors to Paros, which is a beautiful island between Mykonos and Santorini. That means my granddaughters have English, Scottish and Greek blood in them. When I'm out and about in London I mix with people from all over the world and I'm all for people being allowed into Britain who assimilate, work hard and love the country. Those kinds of people, wherever they're from, should be welcomed with open arms.

When I was growing up, I had absolutely no interest in what was going on in the world, because I was so into my football. I barely even remember the Vietnam War happening. But now, if anything major happens, I'll be glued to it for days. And I like to see it from all angles, which might mean flicking between Al Jazeera, CNN and France 24 (not so much the BBC, which seems to have lost its way).

When the Scottish independence referendum took place in 2014, I couldn't stop watching stuff about it. I'd finish the show, head back to my flat in Canary Wharf and watch the coverage all afternoon, even though I wasn't allowed to vote. How bonkers is that? I played for Scotland in a World Cup and I've been disenfranchised because I've lived in England too long. Not that I would have voted for independence, which will dismay a lot of my old mates. Like most Scottish people, I regard myself as a Scot rather than a Brit. But I was pleased the vote went the way it did because I think Scotland is stronger in the union. The independence plan seemed to rely a great deal on North Sea oil for wealth, and they didn't seem to have a plan B if oil revenues collapsed, which they have in the past. But now Nicola Sturgeon is taking Scotland back down the same path, because the SNP are absolutely intent on taking us out of the UK. That's a mistake, because it wouldn't make Scotland a better nation. It would have an awful lot of pride and heart but it would be in all sorts of trouble financially.

Despite being born in Govan and growing up in a semi-detached house in Simshill, I vote Conservative. Some of my fellow Glaswegians will no doubt call me a traitor and a sell-out, just as they did with Rod, but it honestly doesn't bother me. I'm my own man and I don't care if people disagree with me. One day I was having a drink in Paddy Crerand's pub and we fell into a discussion about politics. Paddy is from the Gorbals, the same as my dad, and staunch Labour. So when he asked me if I voted for my country or my family, and I replied that I voted for my family, Paddy went mad. He thought I was totally out of order, because as far as he was concerned the country came first. I said to him, 'Paddy, I take your point, but I'm a grown man and can vote how I like.'

I understand why people from poorer parts of the country might hate the idea of being run by posh people from London. These politicians have nothing in common with them, because they're all educated at top schools and top universities and previously worked as lawyers and bankers. But people have to look at the bigger picture. Labour are always trying to sell this utopian dream, of a country where the wealth is divided equally and everything is wonderful. But there was no way I could have voted for Corbyn and his sidekick John McDonnell at the last couple of elections, because they were utterly clueless. I'm not Boris Johnson's biggest fan, but Labour would have spent too much money and dropped us back in the shit, like they always do.

It's often assumed that people with a few quid don't vote Labour because of a fear they'll put up taxes, but it's got nothing to do with that, at least in my case. I just don't think Labour are fit to run the country. Every time we've had a Labour government they've wasted the country's wealth. Then when the Tories get back in they have to pick up the pieces and try to put everything back together again, which means they can get nothing else done.

Ever since I was a kid, I wanted to better myself. Instead of getting the bus, I wanted my own car. Once I had my own car, I wanted a better car. Then I wanted to buy my own house, and once I had my own house, I wanted a better house. Then when I had a family, I wanted my kids to have better than I'd had growing up. Hopefully they'll do the same for their kids. I don't see what's wrong with that. That kind of opportunity stems from having a stable economy, and I think the Tories are more likely to provide that than Labour.

I know a lot of kids don't have a lot of support growing up, but if you're clever enough and determined enough you can achieve your goal. I know this because so many of my old mates from Glasgow, people who had humble upbringings not much different from mine, have achieved incredible things. I make no bones about how fortunate I've been. But I don't agree with this notion that people are trapped in poverty by a Tory government. There is always a way out. If I was a youngster with a job I hated, working in a factory or a call centre, I'd be thinking, 'I can't be doing this for another thirty or forty years. How do I get out of here? Because I have to get out of here.'

You can't just accept your fate, you've got to fight. I know it's far easier said than done, but people from deprived backgrounds have been making a success of themselves for hundreds of years. They had ambition and they took a chance, instead of following the herd and saying, 'I suppose this is what I am for the rest of my days. I'll never be a success and lead a nice comfortable life.'

If I was in charge of the country, top of my list of things to solve would be bureaucratic wastage and homelessness. People say the NHS has been neglected by the Tories, but I'm not sure that's the case. There is just so much waste in the NHS, including too many managers clogging things up in the middle. I feel for the nurses and doctors and other front-line workers who just want to do their job without all the red tape. Someone needs to go in with an iron fist and say, 'No, we're not doing it like this any more. We need to cut this and cut that and let the front-line workers do their jobs without interference.'

The amount of homelessness on our streets makes me very sad. Whenever I drive into London I'll stop at the same petrol station to fill the car up and there will always be the same homeless guy out the front, under a blanket. It doesn't matter if it's a freezing cold January morning or if it's been pouring with rain, he'll always be there. Where my flat is in Canary Wharf there are rough sleepers everywhere, and that's the financial heart of the country. I'll buy them a sandwich or a packet of biscuits instead of giving them money, and I'll sometimes look at them and think, 'What happened? How did they get into that state? Were they hard done by? Or was there nothing anyone could have done to help them? How long will they live? Can anyone do anything to save them, or is their fate already sealed?' Sometimes I won't be able to stop thinking about it for the rest of the day.

I don't know how we solve homelessness, but it's embarrassing that there's so much of it in a great country like the United Kingdom. Whoever is in power needs to get a grip on it. Maybe the government should compel some of these massive foreign companies that duck out on tax to pay a homeless tax instead. Because by ducking out on tax, they're contributing to the problem. If the government said 'Come on, it's not a lot of money, in fact it's peanuts to you lot', they couldn't really say no. Surely they'd be shamed into doing something? It's not like they don't know it's going on, because they have homeless people sleeping in the doorways of their offices all over the country.

I'm a doer more than a thinker. I don't see obstacles, I see possibilities, opportunities. We need a government that sees things the same way, especially in a post-Brexit world. Once coronavirus restrictions are fully lifted, I hope the current lot will hit the ground running and start getting things done.

11

Here for a Visit

I was never able to replace the thrill of scoring a goal. Netting in front of your own fans, or in front of the Stretford End at Old Trafford or the Kop at Anfield (right foot, top corner), is the best feeling anyone can have. But when you walk around my house, you won't see much evidence that I ever played football.

Don't get me wrong, I've got great memories of my football career and do have the odd reminder on display. In my study you'll see four football pictures: of me winning the UEFA Cup with Ipswich and Spurs, of me and the Manchester United squad, and of Billy McNeill leading Celtic out for the 1967 European Cup final. There's also a framed Celtic shirt signed by five of the Lisbon Lions, with '67' and 'Brazil' on the back. I'll treasure that for as long as I live. I still have my Scotland caps, medals, match balls, programmes and the scrapbooks my mum and dad used to put together, but I've no idea where they are. Beyond my study, our house is a football-free zone.

Sometimes, someone will send me a clip of me scoring a goal and I won't have seen it for decades. When I was invited to Singapore to give that speech at the cricket club they showed a video of some of my goals, a few of which I'd never seen, including an overhead kick for Spurs against Manchester United. But lovely as it is to be reminded that I was a half-decent player back in the day, I prefer to live in the present rather than constantly reminisce.

Mike Parry recently told a journalist that I was a better broadcaster than I was a footballer. Porky knows nothing about football, so I'd take his opinion with a pinch of salt. But it was very kind of him to say so. I played for my country in a World Cup, so I wasn't bad at football. But I haven't done badly at broadcasting either. To pick it up without any training and do it for twenty years is something I'm proud of. And when I know I've done a great show, when I'm in no doubt that my listeners enjoyed it, the feeling comes close to scoring a goal.

Not that I've been garlanded with awards for my efforts in broadcasting. Some years, talkSPORT didn't even enter the Sony Awards (now known as the Radio Academy Awards) because tables for the event at the Grosvenor House Hotel were so expensive and the BBC won everything anyway. But in 2011 the bosses booked two tables, amid lots of whispers that we might win something for a change. My co-presenter Ronnie Irani was very excited about our chances, but as soon as I found out which table we were sitting on I knew we weren't winning anything: while the programme director Moz Dee was on a table next to the stage, me and Ronnie were on a table right at the back, next to the bins. And when it was announced that 5 Live's Danny

Baker had won the award for best breakfast show, I headed straight for the exit.

But three years later I was inducted into the Radio Academy Hall of Fame, alongside legends such as Terry Wogan, Jimmy Young, Tony Hancock, Alan Freeman and the Goons. Everyone who's anyone in radio was at the induction lunch at the Savoy, and it was nice for someone who didn't work for the BBC to get recognized for a change. My wife and kids came along, and one of the nicest things was being congratulated by other presenters. Trevor Nelson said he listened a lot and Jo Whiley told me her dad was a big fan.

I've often felt like an outsider in the industry, but not that day. That said, awards aren't important in the grand scheme of things. What's important is enjoying what I do and bringing in big numbers over a long period of time.

In June 2019, I celebrated my sixtieth birthday by broadcasting the show from my local pub in Suffolk, followed by a four-day party at my house. My brother came over from Australia, and Ally McCoist, Ray Parlour and my old Spurs mate Paul Miller were there, along with scores of others. We had a sensational time, and despite the milestone birthday, I wasn't thinking about retirement or winding down. But broadcasting is a ruthless world. Just like football, you rarely go out on your own terms. And sure enough, when new management took over at talkSPORT, they suggested that twenty years was a long time to have been doing my job and that I should cut back on my shows.

That was a bit of a shock, and I'd be a liar if I said I wasn't disappointed. The bosses also knew I was pissed off. When you present a breakfast radio show for that long, you have highs and lows. When it's summer and it's warm and light early, it's not too difficult to roll out of bed at 4 a.m.; when it's winter, it's cold and dark and chucking it down, and you know you've got to drive 100 miles to London, it's not so great. Some weeks I was doing six days a week – the breakfast show Monday to Friday and another show on Saturday with Mike Parry – and that starts to grind you down. But I was still enjoying it so much and my most recent quarterly listening figures were the best I'd ever had.

At the same time, I understood where the bosses were coming from. They needed to plan for the future and didn't think it was fair to give a new presenter only one or two shows a week. I think the world of Laura Woods, who is now doing Mondays to Wednesdays, and I genuinely hope she goes from strength to strength. It's a tough gig, but she's more than up to the task.

I didn't like it at first, mooching about the house when I thought I should have been in the studio. But I soon got over the disappointment and started feeling reinvigorated. I don't have to set an alarm every night now and really look forward to work. My challenge is to make my two shows the best of the week, not only on talkSPORT but also on radio as a whole. I've also got the big events to look forward to, whether it's the Cheltenham Festival (yep, they're still sending me!), the Grand National, the Ryder Cup or the football World Cup. I'm certainly not giving up, don't worry about that. I've got plenty more to give.

My wife was happy that I was winding down a bit – until coronavirus came along. At the start of lockdown in March 2020 it was a bit of a novelty spending so much time together and we got on like a house on fire. But after a while I'm sure she was thinking, 'I hope he gets another job when this is all over.'

I thought I might spend most of lockdown whingeing about being cooped up. But I loved it at first, sitting in the garden with a glass of wine and walking our puppy Hugo in the beautiful Suffolk countryside. I drove about four times in three months, twice to the shops and twice to the garden centre. Jill does most of the hard jobs around the house and garden because my back is useless and my knees have gone, but at least I was able to lend a hand. I was in charge of barbecues and getting to know the neighbours over the garden wall.

When I started getting a bit bored, I did some podcasts with my old mate Porky; then my daughter Lucy suggested I kill some time by recording a podcast of my own. I told her I didn't want to talk about football, so she suggested I talk about wine, with the odd football story thrown in. That sounded like a plan, because people are always asking me about my favourite tipples.

I'm into wine in the same way I'm into horseracing. I don't claim to be Oz Clarke, and I'm not one of these people who thinks wine can only be good if it's expensive. But I love finding out where they're from, all about the grapes and the soil they're grown in. I love wandering around vineyards, whether in France or Spain, and am friends with wine producers from all over the world.

The first couple of podcasts were downloaded by about ten thousand people and all the emails and tweets from listeners gave me a bit of a lift during lockdown. Even better than that, I was being sent cases of wine from all over the country.

Because the weather was beautiful at the start of lockdown, I got reacquainted with Whispering Angel, which is a beautiful Provence rosé. It's pale, crisp and fresh and perfect for summer drinking. I associate Whispering Angel with some of my favourite times and it often comes to my rescue when things aren't looking too promising. Once, we were visiting the island of Antiparos, which is a short ferry ride from Paros (where my daughter's father-in-law has a couple of beautiful villas). Don't get me wrong, Greek wine is OK, but when I walked into this beach bar and saw Whispering Angel on the menu, I said to my wife, 'You're driving today . . .'

Another time, a mate took me to a beach bar called La Sala by the Sea in Puerto Banus. It was a bit too *Love Island* for my liking and not my cup of tea at all, full of tanned hunks walking about with their tops off and girls with everything hanging out. But once I had a glass of Whispering Angel in my hand I felt completely chilled and transported to another place.

I first got into red wine when Ipswich played Roma in the UEFA Cup in 1982. We went out for a bit of food before the game and I tried a couple of glasses of Barolo, which is a beautiful heavy red (I'm not sure what our goalkeeper Paul Cooper was drinking, but he had a shocker and we lost 3-0). When it comes to red, the heavier the better, I say. There's nothing more satisfying than sitting in front of a roaring fire with a bottle of Barolo or Amarone, which is another punchy red from Valpolicella, and some rib-eye steak or cheese.

I wound the podcast up when lockdown started easing, but I'll never stop enjoying wine. If there is a heaven, I reckon it might consist of drinking vino at the races with the family. Can it get any better?

I wouldn't say I worry about getting old. I try not to think about it and take each day as it comes. But when I hit sixty, it became more difficult to ignore. My body started aching a little bit more, especially in the winter, when the cold gets to the old football injuries. Some mornings my ankles ache, my knees ache, my hips ache, my back aches, and I'll have a familiar twinge in my Achilles. I've also got to watch my chest, because I've had pneumonia twice and bronchitis several times. I put that down to the dampness when I was growing up in Glasgow, because my mum had the same problem.

In 2014 I had an operation that almost went horribly wrong. After fourteen years behind the mic, speaking almost non-stop for four hours a day, five and sometimes six days a week, I'd started having one or two problems with my throat. I was sent to a specialist, who put a scope down my neck and saw a few things that concerned him.

A few weeks later I went in for surgery. I remember being wheeled into theatre, given an anaesthetic and joking with the nurses, before waking up and saying, 'How did it go?' The nurse fetched the surgeon, and when he turned up he said, 'Mr Brazil, we didn't carry out the operation because you stopped breathing. We had to revive you rather quickly.' It was a bit scary to think I might have died on that operating table, but I have a fatalistic outlook on life. When your time's up, it's up.

I'm overweight, I drink too much, and I don't do any exercise. My wife and daughters are always telling me to stop going out, stop drinking and get fit. I listen to what they have to say and mull it over. But I'm too set in my ways to change my lifestyle, and it would just make me miserable. I'm happy with my body and how I feel, I really am. I can't think of anything better than sitting in my garden with a glass of red wine, looking at the glorious countryside. But I don't want to go running or cycling in it.

There will come a time when I'll have to slow down, maybe if I start getting ill all the time, but at the moment I feel OK. The fact I'm now getting a lot more sleep, what with only working two days a week for talkSPORT, has got to help. I listened to a podcast recently, about sleep deprivation and how it can knock years off your life. That made me think, 'Blimey, maybe cutting back happened at just the right time.' That said, I've known too many people who looked after themselves all their lives and squirrelled their money away only to drop down dead out of the blue. How depressing is that?

I'd be lying if I said money didn't make me happy. When you grow up with not a lot, you crave nice things as an adult. And when you've had money and lost it, like I have a couple of times, it hammers home how important it is. But unlike my parents, who saved every penny, I like to spend. I should certainly have a lot more money than I have, but I've got enough to have a good life.

I can never see myself retiring completely because I'm not one for sitting in front of a fire with a rug over my legs, and if people are still willing to pay me for podcasts, lunches and dinners, I'd be daft to turn them down. I don't have an agent, just as I never had an agent when I was playing football. My daughter Michelle helps out a bit. She'll say, 'Someone's been in touch, they want you to do such and such.' And if I'm happy with the deal, I'll do it. If I'm not, I won't. But most of my speaking work comes via word of mouth. Ray Parlour, who's a great after-dinner speaker himself, will often call and say he's recommended me to someone, and I'll often do the same for him. I could be doing three or four speaking engagements a week, but if I do one, I'm happy. People sometimes say to me, 'You're mad, you could have got double that.' And I reply, 'It doesn't matter, I'm happy with what they've given me.'

But the combination of cutting back to two days a week and the lockdown allowed me to ponder what life might be like when I do finally hang up the microphone. As well as a lovely house in Suffolk, we've got a little property near Marbella which we use quite a lot. It's not some mansion in Puerto Banus, it's just a little town house. We can jump on a plane, go there for three or four days, recharge our batteries in the sun, and I play a little bit of golf. Just perfect. We've also got a motorhome, which I'd love to get more use out of. I'm dying to go up to the Scottish Highlands and over to the west coast of Ireland.

Being able to afford nice things makes all the hard work seem worth it. And it's lovely to be able to help your kids buy their first car or house, as well as friends who might be having a hard time. But growing up in Glasgow and playing football in the seventies and eighties also gave me a sense of perspective. I've got friends who don't have as much money as me but are very happy. Other friends have much more money than me and seem miserable. Everyone is different.

That's why it pisses me off when I hear footballers whingeing about not feeling appreciated and wanting to move to another club for more money. These people are delusional. Nowadays, a top player is made for life after a few years in the Premier League. At least they should be, if they're given good advice and they invest their money wisely. There are people out there in the real world struggling to put food on the table, and I have old friends who played at the highest level who are scratching around trying to make a living. Others have fallen ill and don't have the money to look after themselves. My old Ipswich team-mate Kevin Beattie, one of the greatest English players of his generation, died skint. I think of these people and realize how lucky I've been, and it does my head in that so many modern footballers don't think the same.

But never mind money, family is the most important thing in life. I married Jill in 1981, on a snowy day in Ipswich. Ipswich is only a small place, so we would bump into each other in various bars and restaurants. She had a lovely family and her dad was a big fan of Ipswich Town. He had a private box and loved coming to away games, places like London and Manchester. It wasn't a long courtship, because we hit it off immediately. To be honest, us getting married was never in doubt.

But it takes a certain kind of woman to put up with being married to a man like me. When I was playing football, Jill had to follow me from club to club. Well, she didn't have to do anything, but she did it without complaint. That meant leaving her home and family in Suffolk and making new homes in Hertfordshire, Cheshire and Switzerland. Then when I started presenting my show on talkSPORT she was suddenly married to a man who was hardly ever at home. Until I cut back to two shows a week, I'd disappear in the early hours of Monday morning and be in London until Friday. Then when I returned to Suffolk I'd like to catch up on what had been going on. As you can imagine, that didn't always go down well.

One day I mentioned on the show that Jill wakes me up on a Monday morning with a cup of coffee and a slice of toast before nipping outside, starting my car up and scraping the frost off my windscreen. I wasn't joking, and what's wrong with that? As far as I'm concerned, that's just a nice thing for a wife to do. I didn't order her to do it, I didn't even ask her to do it, she did it out of the goodness of her heart.

Anyway, someone from the TV programme *Loose Women* must have been listening, because the following day they all gave me a pasting and concluded that I was a male chauvinist dinosaur. The only person who stood up for me was Stacey Solomon. A couple of days later, Mike Parry brought it up on the show, and I pointed out that the *Loose Women* weren't exactly experts on marriage because they'd been divorced about twelve times between them. Jill went mad, because she watches *Loose Women*. She said to me, 'You shouldn't say that about them!'

'Bollocks! They slagged me off, so I'm entitled to stand up for myself. Plus, they were making out you were an idiot for putting up with me.'

'Hmmm, they might have a point . . .'

In all seriousness, the fact that we haven't lived in each other's pockets, like a lot of couples do, is probably why our marriage has lasted for thirty-nine years and counting.

My daughters have done great for themselves. Before she had kids, Michelle organized events for big companies in the City, and she now does a bit of work for me. My middle daughter Lucy is a senior designer for the Radley handbag company, and my youngest, Stephanie, is a doctor who spent most of lockdown battling coronavirus in Ipswich Hospital. That was worrying, because she didn't have the right equipment to do the job in the early days, but I was also incredibly proud of her, as I am her two sisters.

None of what my daughters have achieved has had anything to do with me, because I'm just a footballer who became a broadcaster. We brought them up well, I loved to treat them, and Jill still cooks and cleans for them. But they worked hard for their success. And what makes me most happy is that they're happy.

I've been dealt good cards, no doubt about that. I had an immensely enjoyable career as a footballer, a job every boy grows up wanting to do. I've now been chatting for a living for two decades, which doesn't seem like a job most of the time. I've travelled the world and met thousands of brilliant people. I've got a great wife, three wonderful kids and three beautiful grandchildren. I'm one of the lucky ones, and I'm going to keep enjoying myself until I can't. My favourite saying is 'We're only here for a visit.' I really believe that, and I want to make the most of it.

Alan Brazil is a Scottish broadcasting legend and former football player, most notably for Ipswich Town, Tottenham Hotspur, Manchester United and internationally for Scotland. He played as a forward before being forced to retire due to a recurring back injury.

After retirement, Alan moved into media presentation, initially on television, before a career in radio where for many years he has presented the Alan Brazil Sports Breakfast show on talkSPORT.